A TRAILS BOOKS

GREAT
WISCONSIN
TAVERNS

OVER 100 DISTINCTIVE BADGER BARS

DENNIS BOYER

TRAILS BOOKS
Black Earth, Wisconsin

Library of Congress Catalog Card Number: 2002109056
ISBN: 1-931599-18-1

Editor: Stan Stoga
Cover designer: Kathie Campbell
Cover photograph: Mark Lepinske
Part illustrations: Owen Coyle

Printed in the United States of America by Sheridan Books.

08 07 06 05 04 03 02   5 4 3 2

Trails Media Group, Inc.
P.O. Box 317 · Black Earth, WI 53515
(800) 236-8088 · e-mail: books@wistrails.com
www.trailsbooks.com

In Memory of the
Pinckney Street Hideaway,
Mother's Pub,
Cafe Melange,
Four Mile House,
Thunder Road,
and the pre-fire Crystal Corner

▼ ▼ ▼ ▼ ▼ ▼ ▼ ▼ ▼ ▼ ▼ ▼ ▼ ▼ ▼ ▼ ▼ ▼

Contents

▼   ▼   ▼   ▼   ▼   ▼   ▼   ▼   ▼   ▼   ▼   ▼   ▼   ▼   ▼   ▼   ▼   ▼   ▼

Introduction

One could easily conclude that the compilation of an abridged Wisconsin tavern guide is the height of presumption. Wisconsin's 14,000-plus licensed establishments give the Badger state an incredible range of choices and settings. Our diverse ethnic mix and varied cultural landscape give us virtually every North American tavern variation except the Mississippi Delta juke joint (although a few Wisconsin places adopt some southern features). Even some facsimile western saloons and southwestern cantinas weigh in with in-use hitching rails and weather-beaten sombreros.

This range provides one of the chief challenges to pulling a guide together when space allows but for a hundred or so entries rather than thousands. In addition, the question of what is a tavern is not a settled matter. All manner of establishments serve beer and other alcoholic beverages. Some spots stretch our traditional vision of the tavern. Others playfully and creatively fuse tavern elements in a variety of hospitality settings.

My working definition of tavern—assembled in the process of compiling this guidebook and after much consultation with tavern sources— has as much to do with sociology as with physical setting and business structure. First and foremost, a tavern is a location in which regular patrons gather to share drinks and fellowship. This element of community is what gives the tavern its continuity with the *stube* in Germany and the pub in Ireland.

Most of us also expect a tavern to have a bar counter of some sort, with stools after a fashion. Some would be so particular as to say that an establishment is not a true tavern without a massive back bar, replete with mirrors, oak columns, and a reproduction of the famous dogs-cheating-at-poker painting. Others, of the minimalist school, require only cold beer, brandy, and a rough plank on which to sit or lean.

This guidebook adopts a great deal of elasticity in the definition of taverns. A few establishments included here might lack elements that purists deem essential. But all have that key ingredient of a regular crowd that gathers for socializing and imbibing. And, a few comments regarding subculture and rough language notwithstanding, all are places in which a new face is welcome.

Honesty compels an admission of what this guide is *not*. It is not an attempt to rank Wisconsin taverns. It is impossible to use the standards by which one might evaluate fine restaurants. Taverns included here are great Wisconsin taverns, but an effort to rank them is an exercise in the mathematics of apples and oranges— even though I couldn't resist taking a stab at a "Top Ten" list (see page 10). Rankings based solely on amenities, food, and beer selection would skew the guidebook toward southeast Wisconsin. An effort is made to achieve the geographic balance that will be helpful to the traveler. The entries are organized by the standard quadrants used by the Wisconsin Department of Tourism. To avoid a hint of favoritism, I organized the taverns within each quadrant in alphabetical order of the city or town in which they are located. Readers will detect, however, that I have my preferences (most "blues clubs" outside Milwaukee manage to squeeze into this guidebook).

Twenty years of travel throughout Wisconsin took me to about 2,000 taverns before I started this project. I visited about 300 more in the two years of compiling the guide. Many of the spots evoke warm memories of friends made and local legends told. While I may have grown fussier in preferences over the years, I can still report that I liked almost all of the taverns. My tavern journals contain only a few disparaging notations such as "should be burned, bulldozed, and turned into a parking lot."

The passage of time has brought many changes to the tavern industry. Simple ownership of a Wisconsin tavern is no longer a guaranteed license to print money. Regulatory burdens, drinking age changes, and tougher drunk-driving enforcement all combine to make life more complicated for the tavern owner. Many tavern owners feel that Native American gaming in the form of casinos has also diverted business. I saw no evidence of this, and by and large, the casino crowd is not a tavern crowd.

Another thing I noticed on my travels are the parallels between the tavern industry and Wisconsin's dairy farms. One major similarity is age demographics. Many owner/operators in both sectors are of retirement age. Some continue because of a genuine fondness for their vocation. Others hang on bitterly in the usually vain hope that if they wait, a sucker with wads of cash will show up to buy them out.

Chain or franchise tavern/restaurants also pop up to fuel the insecurity of mom-and-pop taverns. While none of the franchise places are included in the guide, it must be conceded that they generally do a good job. In our modern mobile society they fulfill the needs of those without community roots and those who like the comfortable guarantee that the setting will be similar in each location.

All the troubling trends aside, it could still be argued that Wisconsin is in the midst of a golden age of taverns and beer drinking. Young progressive owners have revitalized many a moribund spot. Places that stress customer satisfaction are thriving. The spread of microbreweries and brew pubs has done much to educate consumers. Indeed, the buildup of Wisconsin brew pubs, the number of which tripled in the last two years, complicated my guidebook task by threatening to displace the listings of more traditional rustic spots. I've attempted to recognize these newer establishments by reviewing some, in addition to compiling all of them in a separate list (see page 98). All are worthy of a visit.

A word is in order about beer terminology used in the guidebook. The terms *nationals, standards,* and *industrials* are used to describe the availability of the big brands like Miller and Budweiser. The label *regional* is meant to include Wisconsin's enduring hometown breweries such as Joseph Huber, Stevens

▼ ▼ ▼ ▼ ▼ ▼ ▼ ▼ ▼ ▼ ▼ ▼ ▼ ▼ ▼ ▼ ▼ ▼

Point, and Leinenkugel. The terms *microbrew* and *micros* embrace the brews from the specialty breweries devoted to the production of fine beers and ales in smaller batches. The term *craft brew* is used to denote the specialty beer produced by the larger breweries.

As happens with a project of this type, conditions change and businesses evolve or die. Follow-up efforts caught a few taverns that have closed or changed beyond recognition. Undoubtedly, there are tavern gems that escaped my attention. Updates, additions, and notice of significant changes from readers are welcome and can be sent to Trails Media Group, P.O. Box 317, Black Earth, WI 53515.

Enjoy your tavern tours of Wisconsin. Our taverns are a unique part of our heritage and landscape. Cheers!

▼ ▼ ▼ ▼ ▼ ▼ ▼ ▼ ▼ ▼ ▼ ▼ ▼ ▼ ▼ ▼ ▼ ▼ ▼

Acknowledgments

I n the first edition I gave a nod of thanks to those who inhabited the taverns of my past. Those acknowledgments provided the reader with hints that the author's view of taverns was formed over the span of three-plus decades and over a four continent reach. Those words of thanks gave proof that my view of the tavern is one heavily informed by the blue collar world of railworkers, military noncommissioned officers, loggers, construction workers, and farmers.

When I sent the first edition draft to Trails Books I had seen the innards of approximately 2,000 of Wisconsin's 14,000 taverns. Since then I have visited about 500 more taverns. It continues to amaze me that I am still finding novel and attractive things in these gathering spots. It continues to delight me that I find many old acquaintances deepened and many new ones inspired by our Wisconsin tavern habitat. Write as I might about beers, amenities, and locations, the narrative of taverns it all comes down to people.

Here are some of the people who provided companionship and comment during the "field research" leading up to the second edition: John Bergum, Bill Boyer, Ronnie Boyer, Conrad Amenhauser, Andrea Dearlove, Bob Kasper, Susan Lampert Smith, Jeff Platt, Jennifer Grondin, Kevin Traas, Tom Dwyer, Dave Johnson, Pat James, Pat Halpin, Stu Becker, Eric Griffiths, Rob Rule, Dave Cieslewicz, Carla Shedivy, Johna Roth, Sue Peterson, Jeff Donoghue, Keith Daniels, Linda Wong, Roy de la Rosa, Phil Neuenfeldt, Jamie Ciccoli, Sam Johnson, Lisa Hoffman, Don Waukau, Stacey Lang, Mary Devitt, John Huber, Kirby Fredericks, Bean Prettie, Tom Nelson, Kurt Schultz, Rick Borowitz, Johanna Meyer, Tom Thornton and last, but certainly not least, my sudsing buddy of over twenty years, Owen Coyle.

Thanks to all of you. May we share many a pint in the portion of the great tavern tour that lies ahead.

Thanks also to Trails Books for recognizing taverns as an indispensable part of Wisconsin culture.

Finally, to Donna Weikert, thanks for the emotional and logistical support. Couldn't have done it without you.

Southeast Wisconsin

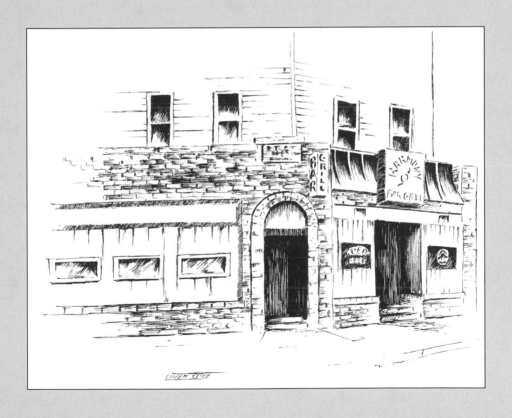

▼ ▼ ▼ ▼ ▼ ▼ ▼ ▼ ▼ ▼ ▼ ▼ ▼ ▼ ▼ ▼ ▼ ▼ ▼

Make no mistake about it, the southeast section of the state is prime tavern country. Sure, the mention of Wisconsin might evoke an image of log taverns on mist-shrouded lakes. But southeast Wisconsin is the land of *Happy Days* and the Fonz, beers that made Milwaukee famous, machine shops, and is the home of Harley-Davidson, and a healthy mix of Holsteins, cheese factories, and small towns.

It is also one of the most ethnically German areas in North America. Before Prohibition it was a stronghold of local breweries that found homes in almost every community with more than a thousand people. It was also home to great brewing fortunes that left legacies in Milwaukee.

Some would say that southeast Wisconsin's peak tavern period came in the prosperous 1950s and 1960s when industrial giants like Allis-Chalmers, Caterpillar, and American Motors provided tens of thousands of decent-paying jobs. Neighborhood taverns thrived, as did the taverns across from plant gates and in or near the union halls. Entertainment options had not expanded to today's level and the generation gap had not created tavern turf wars. Live music was common in tavern venues and ranged from polkas to country and western to brand-new rock and roll. A generation of World War II veterans, flush with the happy swagger of taming a world gone mad, celebrated survival and hope for the future.

Wisconsin's tavern landscape changed with the social and economic changes of the 1970s and 1980s. Younger patrons sought out places where long hair and colorful clothing would not invite harassment. Many older taverns were remodeled as lounges and discos that drew upon urban nightclub traditions. Decline of heavy industry and creeping rust belt malaise cut heavily into the disposable income and optimism of the blue-collar sector.

These changes notwithstanding, the area is still one of the best places in North America to drink beer and visit taverns. Indeed, with its proliferation of brew pubs, spiffed-up microbrew bars, and rediscovered classic neighborhood taverns, one could easily conclude that southeast Wisconsin is the heartland of a tavern renaissance.

As with the other areas demarked by the Wisconsin Department of Tourism's regional divisions, the southeast part of the state presents a varied cultural geography. The lakeshore district of Sheboygan and Manitowoc closely resembles the industrial/maritime clusters one finds in parts of Michigan and Ohio. Milwaukee, of course, is as close as we get to big-city feel. Madison is in a category by itself as a government and academic center. The Lake Winnebago area, particularly the eastern shore, has a unique subculture of fishing and boating taverns. Throw in Kenosha, Racine, Janesville, and zones as varied as Lake Geneva, Wisconsin Dells, and Horicon Marsh, and you have a microcosm of the Upper Midwest.

Milwaukee and Madison could easily provide a sufficient number of notable taverns to merit guidebooks of their own. Both cities pose challenges to the compiler of a statewide guide by offering enough unique and well-appointed taverns to threaten to squeeze out rural and small-town taverns. Growing numbers of taverns in both cities pay close heed to contemporary consumer preferences. Both communities have many neighborhoods worthy of pub crawls.

Driving tours of rural taverns are not as compact or linear as in much of the rest of the state. The four-lane highways displaced many of the old roadhouses, while malls and suburban housing transformed the settings around others. Some travelers still favor the many rural and small-town taverns off the side roads of Highway 51 in Columbia County. Others prefer the Cambridge-Jefferson-Waukesha stretch of Highway 18. A unique trek in ice fishing season can be found on segments of Highways 151 and 55 that hug Lake Winnebago between Fond du Lac and Sherwood. So whether you're in the mood for big-city adventures or small-town hospitality (or anything in between), the southeast region has it all.

▼ ▼ ▼ ▼ ▼ ▼ ▼ ▼ ▼ ▼ ▼ ▼ ▼ ▼ ▼ ▼ ▼ ▼

Beloit

Suds O'Hanahan's Irish Pub
435 E. Grand Avenue
(608) 368-1933

Rock County is just starting to catch up with the beer craze and much of the education is occurring at Suds O'Hanahan's. At one time, Beloit had many more pleasant neighborhood taverns, but some neighborhoods have varying degrees of decay and the stressed-out bars have been slow to pick up on beer diversity. Still, there is a fine tavern tradition in Beloit that this pub manages to at once uphold and update.

Suds O'Hanahan's coolers hold a treasure of 50 bottled imports and domestics, with some emphasis as you might expect on the Emerald Isle. After a concession or two to our national brews, the taps give a tip of the hat in the same geographical direction, with Harp, Bass, and Guinness proudly flowing. The diverse crowd pulls in for sandwiches and snacks, too. The regulars include many border hoppers from Illinois. Many beer fanciers are drawn in by positive mentions of Suds O'Hanahan's on pub crawl websites and various beer-related publications. It's a worthy spot in Wisconsin's southern border county.

Our hardy team of tavern inspectors pronounced it their favorite Rock County watering hole on a 22-bar tour that spanned the distance from Edgerton to the Illinois line. It is worth mentioning that I was in the company of two veteran pub crawlers who've done their time at the General Motors assembly plant in Janesville. They related their assessment of tavern health in the area and painted a picture like that encountered in rapidly developing areas like the Fox Valley and Waukesha. They waxed nostalgic about the lost rural taverns and the run-down state of the factory-district bars. They even had a kind word or two to say about the 1960s and 1970s heyday of the area's supper clubs.

Neither of them saw their past favorites reincarnated in the form of Suds's, but they saw in this modern form a lot more hope for the tavern future than we found elsewhere that day. They groused a bit at the lack of places to spit their snuff juice, and they at first uttered snide epithets like "urban hip" and "yuppie beer emporium." Then they settled into the beer, the crowd, and the conversation. They were won over for good when a thirty-something kindergarten teacher explained the distinctions between ale and lager.

Watch out if some of the regulars suggest some spots for you to visit in cross-border South Beloit. Bartenders at Suds's said those forays are definitely a walk on the wild side.

▼ ▼ ▼ ▼ ▼ ▼ ▼ ▼ ▼ ▼ ▼ ▼ ▼ ▼ ▼ ▼ ▼ ▼ ▼

Burnett

Winkers Tap
N8638 Market Street
(920) 689-2348

Winkers is what our mothers used to expect from a mom-and-pop tavern: clean Formica counters and scrubbed floors. On my first visit I sat and watched in awe as they washed the windows. Even the velvet paintings look dry-cleaned! Here is the antithesis of the seedy conditions found in far too many taverns. You know the type I'm referring to: dust on the potato chip bags, peeling linoleum floors, grimy cooking facilities, and restrooms that merit the donning of a chemical/biological warfare suit. Not at Winkers.

One might ask what would bring a traveler to Burnett other than random cruising. Well, for starters it is on the periphery of the Horicon Marsh area. The Wild Goose State Trail passes within fifty yards of the front door. In the summer months the daytime customers are fresh off the trail looking for cold pop and the unusual tavern offering of Schwann's ice cream. Autumn visitors stop for beer, brandy, directions, and reports on the geese.

It's not uncommon for waterfowl hunters to stop in, too. Even the occasional wildlife manager drops in to wet the whistle and ground the goose lore in a dose of scientific fact. Some great seasoned outdoors storytellers were known to frequent this spot at one time. Many have passed on. But there is still the one up-in-years fellow who will recount a 1940s bitter autumn storm, with full dramatic narrative of the deaths of waterfowl hunters caught out on lakes that day. His stories of frostbite, exposure, howling winds, and frozen bodies had me feeling cold enough to order up a brandy on a July afternoon.

While I often bemoan limited beer selections and scant amenities in small taverns, Winkers is living proof of the beauty of simplicity. Miller beer and Pepsi comprise the bulk of refreshments. A short bar is supplemented by a few tables. The old-style jukebox and the pool table are the only rainy-day distractions other than watching the occasional Wisconsin and Southern train rumble by. But it is still a nice fit for those who can't part with their broken-in hiking boots or other things that have grown comfortable and familiar.

Local residents sometimes use Winkers as a starting point before an evening out. On Friday nights, before the trip to the fish fry, a few drinks are in order. Then comes the 100-yard stroll across the trail and the tracks to Theide's Tavern for catfish and Rolling Rock. A nice little tandem visit!

▼ ▼ ▼ ▼ ▼ ▼ ▼ ▼ ▼ ▼ ▼ ▼ ▼ ▼ ▼ ▼ ▼ ▼

Chilton

The Roll Inn (at Rowland's Calumet Brewing Company)
25 N. Madison Street
(920) 849-2534

If you love beer, you must meet Bob Rowland. There are few tavern hosts who rival Bob's congeniality and outright exuberance. What Wisconsin former governor Tommy Thompson is to Badger State boosterism, Bob Rowland is to the cause of good beer. I have not met the *Homo sapiens* who has a bad word to say about him, unless you count the comments that his spouse is even nicer.

Aside from running one of the smallest (and the most off the beaten track) brew pubs in North America, Bob hosts the annual Wisconsin Microbrewers Fest at the Calumet County fairgrounds. His cheerful face is a regular feature at other microbrew events. Some say that a Wisconsin brew fest does not even count if Bob and his beers do not make an appearance.

The pub and brewery are in a former fire station with a sturdy ragtime-era feel. Owner confidence and customer loyalty allow the Roll Inn to offer only their five year-round brews and three seasonals (including a unique rye beer) as on-premise beverages. They underline that straight-up beer statement with an emphatic no-menu stance.

While somewhat of a hidden jewel, the Roll Inn has since its 1990 opening garnered an extensive word-of-mouth following. It has many local regulars but also boasts an incredible draw of outsiders. During my last visit, the vehicles in the parking lot sported license plates from California, Indiana, Ontario, South Dakota, and Utah. Not to mention a stretch limo from Milwaukee with four beer fanatics.

It goes without saying that such a spot, under the auspices of such a warm and knowledgeable host, would brew up some great beer stories. Is the Pope Catholic? Does a bear relieve itself in the woods? Yes, the beer talk is about as deep as it can get on this earthly plane and on occasion transcends the gap between mortal brewers and the angels who guard the blessed beverage.

I am not exaggerating when I say that beer is treated with reverence here. There are thirsty pilgrims who sojourn here who see a sacredness in beer that is positively tribal in its spirituality. One such apostle held me spellbound with a lengthy psalm of beer's connection to ancient rites, shamanism, healing, herbalism, and magic. Before he was done I could experience in a good beer the legacy of druids and medicine men and women. He predicted a time when beer will again be brewed that lets us commune with the Divine. Holy beer stein!

▼ ▼ ▼ ▼ ▼ ▼ ▼ ▼ ▼ ▼ ▼ ▼ ▼ ▼ ▼ ▼ ▼ ▼

Fond du Lac

The Main Pub
6th & Main Streets
(920) 924-7815

Picking a Fond du Lac tavern for this guide proved to be one of the more difficult tasks. This city at the base of Lake Winnebago has an abundance of neighborhood bars and a number of interesting clusters. Part of the difficulty came from the loss of a number of favorites (chief among them the Four Mile House, a venerable roadhouse on Highway 151 south) in the last few years. When a tavern that's been under your skin for two decades bites the dust it's like losing an old friend. But it also reminds you that your friendship with that one spot has kept you out of circulation.

In Fond du Lac, that meant a fresh reconnaissance mission to the downtown Main Street tavern district, an area that a decade ago definitely lacked the easy sociability of the old neighborhood taverns, the character of the west shore fishing bars, and the down-home atmosphere of the country bars on the fringe of the city. Those places are now often closed or have fallen on hard times. It is Main Street that is making a comeback, and the Main Pub is leading the way.

There are very few spots that pack as much in a small space as the Main Pub. It's kind of a narrow dining car configuration, with a bar of generous length and some island-counter seating. Throw in a pool table, two dartboards, a pinball machine, a golf machine, and a massive jukebox and you're in for a tight fit on a crowded weekend night. But if you're over 40 those are nights to avoid anyway, as the average age dips down into the early 20s and is not at all beer savvy considering the on-premises resources. We of the middle years do well to stop in on weekdays after 4 P.M. That's when the crowd is at its diverse best.

And what a nice crowd! The folks lean toward the blue-collar side, with representation of construction workers, local government employees, postal workers, health care employees, and quite a few single parents and older students. Conversations turned up a poet, a few musicians, lots of sports enthusiasts, a couple boaters, and a young Maori woman from New Zealand with a story to tell as warm as her smile.

This is the beer crowd. They account for the coolers stocked with over 50 imports and micros. They prompt the steady pull of the eight taps. The lineups are not exotic but have good representation of various brew types. Of note are the bottles of McEwans Scotch Ale and the oft-tapped Hacker-Pschorr Weisse

▼ ▼ ▼ ▼ ▼ ▼ ▼ ▼ ▼ ▼ ▼ ▼ ▼ ▼ ▼ ▼ ▼ ▼

and Leinie's Berry Weiss. It's also the cigar crowd, with the Don Tomas and Astral brands bearing most of the traffic. Women join in on this puffing, too.

The friendly atmosphere on weekday evenings merits a visit if you're in the area. But the crowd-shy can safely visit on Saturdays before the evening really gets cooking. You might even mix in with a crowd of regulars that forsakes the bar in mid-evening and invites whoever is handy out to a lakeside bonfire.

▼ ▼ ▼ ▼ ▼ ▼ ▼ ▼ ▼ ▼ ▼ ▼ ▼ ▼ ▼ ▼ ▼ ▼

Germania (south of Neshkora)
Longbranch Saloon
W 1936 Eagle Road
(920) 293-8448

A friend called the Longbranch "a quirky curio shop of a bar." While the name conjures up images of Wild West cattle drives and gunfights, the atmosphere is pure Wisconsin marsh country. Speaking of which, the Longbranch squats at the edge of the Germania Marsh State Wildlife Area like a fat bullfrog.

The area is home to some of the strangest ghost stories in the state and has its share of tall tales. One Longbranch regular whispered an odd tale of amorous spirits that visit in the night to consummate their love of living flesh. This account gave new meaning to the phrase "they all look prettier at closing time" and reduced my inclination to take him up on his offer to let me pitch my tent on his spit of land out in the marsh. Another talked of a local variation on Bigfoot. Then there are the fifty-year-old stories of flying saucers. Hey, they're just getting started.

This is home of the "Hippo Burger" and therein lies one of Wisconsin's strangest legends. A decade ago, fishermen in the area were accused of mental disorder and intoxication when they reported seeing a full-grown hippopotamus in local rivers and swamps. It turned out the critter had escaped from a game farm. Ultimately the animal was destroyed after capture efforts failed. Thus the "Hippo Burger." No one is talking if indeed a hippo haunch still occupies a freezer locker.

There is a small colony of Madison East Siders who park RVs and trailers in the area and add to the local color. Just make sure that if any Longbranch storytellers are holding court that they do not turn out to be Madison cabdrivers. They love to pull the chains of casual passersby and act the part of the backwoods yahoo.

While microbrews and imports have not reached into this bit of marsh country, the standard beers are available in around 15 varieties. The locally acclaimed fish fry brings in a mixed crowd of local families, grubby fishermen, and weekend visitors. It's a congenial mixture and is remembered fondly by those whose travels bring them to Germania on an infrequent basis. Kids and adults alike are captivated by the heavily visited bird feeders near an outside deck. Closed Mondays.

▼ ▼ ▼ ▼ ▼ ▼ ▼ ▼ ▼ ▼ ▼ ▼ ▼ ▼ ▼ ▼ ▼ ▼ ▼ ▼

ANOTHER ROUND

Boyer's Top Ten Taverns

Here I go again with the list that launched many a brickbat my way after publication of the first edition. Yes, folks, I said it was a subjective process. Too many beer pontificators took it to be a pure ranking based on industrial specifications. Let me see if I can clear that issue up. Here's where I've had the best gosh darn times since the last edition:

1. Harmony Bar and Grill–Madison
2. New Diggings General Store and Inn–New Diggings
3. Tom's Burned Down Cafe–La Pointe (Madeline Island)
4. Pleasant Ridge Store–Pleasant Ridge (rural Iowa County)
5. Baumgartner's Cheese Store and Tavern–Monroe
6. Witz End–Stevens Point
7. Thai Joe's–Milwaukee
8. Night Hawks–LaCrosse
9. Anchor Bar and Grill–Superior
10. Titletown Brewery–Green Bay

Some would say that this is a list of spots where ladies said suggestive things to me or where astute bartenders observed that I had lost weight and buffed up (it's a relative concept). Maybe there's an element of truth to such claims, but I'd sign an affidavit that these sites are the ones I think of returning to most frequently.

▼ ▼ ▼ ▼ ▼ ▼ ▼ ▼ ▼ ▼ ▼ ▼ ▼ ▼ ▼ ▼ ▼ ▼

Green Lake
The Goose Blind
512 Gold Street
(920) 294-6363

The Goose Blind's management doesn't call attention to its bar area. All the billing goes to its casual dining. Maybe this is a move calculated to keep out the riffraff. Wait a minute, Green Lake has no riffraff! This is definitely not a stop on motorcycle club bar tours. The spot is an entirely modern version of Green Lake's acclaimed Victorian-era hospitality and brings in families from Chicago who maintain fourth- and fifth-generation ties to this resort community.

But it should be a stop on craft brew and microbrew tours. The Goose Blind keeps 12 taps pumping with various brews from Berghoff, Gray's, Sprecher, and Leinenkugel. The bottled-beer list has 30 brands, including many micros and imports. In addition, bartenders get plenty of practice at mixing cocktails. The suds tapper on duty during my last visit claimed to have a repertoire of six different old-fashioneds.

Comfort is the watchword here. No duct-taped barstools; high padded swivel captain's chairs serve the bar. Well-arranged booths and café tables provide additional seating in the bar. A cozy screened-in porch and second-story deck round out the spots to relax. The mood is subdued here, and this is definitely not the type of place where a rebel yell will net you a free drink. Yet the customers are always sociable. It's a suitable place to go for a genteel moment after a stint in a no-holds-barred juke joint.

On a slow day it is often possible to persuade one of the white-haired eminences to talk of that time of wooden rowboats, gentlemen in hats and long-sleeved white shirts rowing, and ivory-skinned ladies hiding beneath parasols. If the stories can be believed, those nineteenth-century ways lasted nearly up to World War II in Green Lake. It's a mood that is still detectable in this community and in this establishment.

Customers range from local professionals to upscale resort patrons. Many are nondrinkers drawn in by the extensive menu. In the bar, the hearty sandwiches, distinctive homemade pizzas, and Mexican specialties keep palates happy.

▼ ▼ ▼ ▼ ▼ ▼ ▼ ▼ ▼ ▼ ▼ ▼ ▼ ▼ ▼ ▼ ▼ ▼

Janesville

Hilltop Pub and Grill
123 E. Milwaukee Street
(608) 758-0809

Janesville represents a mainstream America that might be seen as an update of Norman Rockwell's portrayals of community life. As such, it does not cultivate a reputation as a drinking town, but neither does it harbor the prudish outlook of the previously "dry" communities of nearby southwest Wisconsin.

The Hilltop is a good fit for rock-solid, truck-building Janesville. A well-respected and reasonably priced ($7.95) pot roast dinner, a famous Deluxe Burger, and a mix of national, regional, and local brews make it a favorite spot for both General Motors and government office workers. So it was with some pleasure that this union man was put in a position to argue about both the various regional beers and the major Wisconsin unions. The discussion was fun, but neither dispute was brought to conclusion. That's the beauty of a tavern discussion; it lives for another day and another beer.

Definitely not a "beer snob" bar, the Hilltop serves as a neighborhood tavern for nearby neighborhoods that developed without taverns. It also anchors a downtown that is without a true tavern district. But it is within walking distance of a few other clean and friendly bars. And it should be mentioned that Janesville's taverns are a generally decent lot, even if thought to be too white-bread by two-fisted types and those with a penchant for sleazy gin mills. Hey, this is Janesville.

The Hilltop is a good spot to hear acoustic guitar music. Sometimes there are even performances on weeknights. It's an intimate bar setting with limited seating. So come early on weekend nights. The lively talk about sports, cars, and music is at the bar. Couples, music lovers, and chowhounds occupy the tables. A surprising number of customers here told me that they rarely go into any taverns other than the Hilltop. Even a few Dane County folks are known to slip down to Janesville to relax in this wholesome spot (only in Janesville would the label "wholesome" not act to drive customers away from a tavern).

The big party night of the year is Halloween. It's a Hilltop tradition, with special food and music. Try the "witch's brew." Here the stories are not about ghosts, but about people who partied too hearty and thought they saw ghosts.

▼ ▼ ▼ ▼ ▼ ▼ ▼ ▼ ▼ ▼ ▼ ▼ ▼ ▼ ▼ ▼ ▼ ▼

Kenosha

Brewmasters Brew Pub
4017 80th Street (south of Highway 50)
(262) 694-9050

Brewmasters Northside
1170 22nd Avenue (near UW-Parkside)
(262) 552-2805

OK, I admit it. I'm trying to sneak a few extra watering holes into the guide. But I have a perfect cover for this sneakiness. The businesses are under the same ownership and brew masters. Not to mention that they are twins in the matters of quality and followings. This is a trend that I've failed to note elsewhere: those who get it right in the tavern business are often exactly the right people to open another operation.

My second excuse is that the 80th Street location was the first brew pub in heartland America. At the time of the 1987 opening, on-premises tavern brewing was strictly an East Coast/West Coast phenomenon. We always owe a debt of gratitude to our pioneer forebears.

As if that were not enough to earn Brewmasters a spot in the annals of Wisconsin tavern history, there are the unique circumstances surrounding the start-up at the 22nd Avenue site. Not only is the new brewing facility a state-of-the-art system, but it is infused with Kenosha pride. Dozens of local craftsmen and companies helped with design and set-up. Only in skilled blue-collar Kenosha would you hear steamfitters and machinists mixing beer talk with engineering specifications.

Oh, by the way, the beer also bears the marks of this skill and caring. Over 30 brews are crafted in the course of a year. Few brew pubs approach this variety. Southeast Wisconsin beer fanatics favor the Irish Mocha Stout. My palate was tickled by the Doppelbock. These places have an extremely ambitious brew agenda. But the loyalists, who hail from Burlington, Racine, and northern Illinois, feel that there are more hits than misses. Real trailblazers are always risk takers. Join them in a beer adventure.

Food is also served Kenosha style: calzones, pizzas, pasta, seafood, steaks, brats, and chops. The 80th Street location has a comfortable-shoe feel. The 22nd Avenue site has more bustle, including a 300-seat banquet hall.

▼ ▼ ▼ ▼ ▼ ▼ ▼ ▼ ▼ ▼ ▼ ▼ ▼ ▼ ▼ ▼ ▼ ▼

Kenosha

Ron's Place

3301 52nd Street
(262) 657-5907

Welcome to Wisconsin! This is a frequent introductory stop for our neighboring flatlanders and other visitors to our fair state. Two of the reasons that the fine Illinois folks like to stop in are the good beer and the friendly Wisconsinites. But they keep coming back because of a variety of elements having to do with the Wisconsin tavern mystique. Many such visitors think of Ron's as the traditional urban Wisconsin tavern. It's so much more than that, but why mess with their belief systems? It thankfully is not even a representative Kenosha tavern, many of which came through the 1980s decline a little worse for wear.

Ron's represents that part of Kenosha that bounced back. Some parts did, some didn't. Let's face it, much of Kenosha feels like Illinois. Some even feels like the Bronx. By gosh, you can find Cubs and Bears fans here, and even White Sox fans. White Sox fans! So we can forgive them if they don't know much about Wisconsin north of Highway 11, much less Highway 2.

But Ron's can't be faulted on the beer and hospitality end. They run ten taps balanced with national, regional, and imports. The bottled selection ebbs and flows but seems to always have at least 15 imports. Ron's Place has a reputation for good bartenders and sociable customers. So some of us in Wisconsin reverse the pattern used by Illinois visitors: stop here and take a deep breath before you go on to Chicago.

There's a Madison group that occasionally makes a southeast Wisconsin loop on their way to Cubs games and allows me to ride shotgun on their interstate pub crawl. They are of the belief that it is an absolute ethical necessity to have a last drink at Ron's, in deference to Wisconsin loyalty, to gird their loins against the city masses to the south. They regale the Illinois visitors with bizarre Ed Gein stories and other legends of the Wisconsin wilds. In general they attempt to reinforce every negative stereotype that an urbanite might have about rural life. I hate to break it to them, but I think the city slickers are on to the fact that these Madison "woodsmen" are all desk jockeys with graduate degrees.

▼ ▼ ▼ ▼ ▼ ▼ ▼ ▼ ▼ ▼ ▼ ▼ ▼ ▼ ▼ ▼ ▼ ▼

Madison
Cardinal Bar
418 E. Wilson Street
(608) 251-0800

I n some circles the label "activist hangout" is a dismissive epithet. In Madison it is more likely to suggest lively entertainment and a social conscience. The Cardinal has been a gathering spot for gays and lesbians for years, but its eclectic offerings and the civic activism of owner Ricardo Gonzalez has made it a community institution that is fondly regarded by a host of progressive constituencies. It is difficult to tally the numbers of Madisonians with good things to say about the Cardinal. And for a multitude of reasons.

The Cardinal has hosted countless political fund-raisers and benefits over the last two decades. Yet among nonactivists, the lively nightspot is known more for its dance club side than its politics. Specialty nights are heavy on Latin, swing, and disco. It can be depended on to run early-evening lessons whenever new dance crazes hit town. Celebrity DJs often pick the tunes and get to spin their favorite music for their favorite causes. "Fetish Night" is no longer the local sensation it was when first unleashed, but leather-laden lads and lassies still cut loose and raise the eyebrows of staid passersby.

A classic bar area shows signs of tasteful renovation. Local micros and imports get good billing. Bartenders have a top-notch reputation for cocktails and specialty drinks. The martini drinkers among my circle tell me the Cardinal's is among the best three or four in Madison. Señor Gonzalez's Cuban roots show up in periodic cigar nights.

Madison has lost many of the bars associated with its antiwar glory days. Spots like the now-departed 602 Club were as much a part of the young adulthood of the student movement as the USO and military post clubs were for their parents' generation. The Cardinal is one of the few places where you might run into someone who could tell you about the war at home, the freedom rides, the Madison newspaper strike, and the host of peace and social-justice groups that blossomed in Madison in the 1970s and 1980s. While the level of activism is no longer at the boiling-over point, the Cardinal still reminds many of us of those times when we thought we could change the world and sort of did change it.

Madison

Harmony Bar and Grill
2201 Atwood Avenue
(608) 249-4333

A nalyzed in sociological and folklore journals, praised by restaurant critics, beloved by fans of blues and roots rock, and just plain appreciated by beer drinkers, the Harmony occupies a special niche in Madison's tavern pantheon. It pulls off the trick of serving as a neighborhood tavern and a citywide/regional nightspot. It also bridges the east/west cultural and political divide that is part of life in the capital city. Its status as a favored venue of musicians speaks volumes about the owners' love of the aural arts and about one neighborhood's support of popular culture.

Friday and Saturday nights produce some of the most music-savvy crowds to be found anywhere in Wisconsin. The fans of the bands are about as multigenerational as one would ever see in a music club, often running from those in their twenties to those in their fifties. It is also fairly common for off-duty musicians to drop in to hear the friendly competition. Some fabled blues legends have passed through these doors. As will some legends in the making.

Longtime tavern hoppers may recall several other interesting bar incarnations on this site. The first version was a post-Prohibition family tavern that drew its customers entirely from a few surrounding residential blocks. In 1944, it was reborn as the Karabis Bar, where mixed crowds of Truax Field airmen and Gisholt machinists could be found with ears glued to wartime radio broadcasts. Big-band sounds and FDR's radio chats probably still rattle around in the pressed-tin ceiling. Later came younger blue-collar crowds, and a jukebox replaced the radio.

Reborn again in 1990 as the Harmony Bar and Grill, the spot had the good fortune to fall into the hands of Keith Daniels. The makeover brought seven tap lines and an ever-changing selection of micro and regional draft beer. Bottled beers and mixed drinks are, of course, available if you can pass up the surprises that greet you nearly every time you look at the tap handles.

Then there's the food. The menu does nothing less than redefine tavern food and, like the rotating beer selections, is a constantly expanding universe. The Italian specialties are very well received by patrons. Many say that this sense of fun and experimentation with the menu accounts for a better following among women than most taverns.

Warning to cardplayers: you're in sheepshead fanatic territory. The cardplayers are territorial, though nonthreatening, the few jerks in their numbers being far outweighed by a herd of hail-fellows-well-met. It's a gathering place

▼ ▼ ▼ ▼ ▼ ▼ ▼ ▼ ▼ ▼ ▼ ▼ ▼ ▼ ▼ ▼ ▼

for card-deck devotees so rooted in their affection for the game that they talk of past games as Vikings might recount storied battles. Some of the regulars have even immortalized the games in illustrations and photographs.

▼ ▼ ▼ ▼ ▼ ▼ ▼ ▼ ▼ ▼ ▼ ▼ ▼ ▼ ▼ ▼ ▼ ▼ ▼

Madison

Village Bar
3801 Mineral Point Road
(608) 233-9956

T he Madison tavern scene is not all nightclubs and alternative culture bars. The capitol city is fortunate to have a supply of respectable neighborhood taverns. I can never drive by this place without thinking about the late George Vukelich sitting at a Village Bar table, holding forth on land, politics, and taverns. The Village Bar is thought by many to be the most representative of the west side taverns. It certainly has the most loyal following among the denizens of this land of manicured yards and sculpted hedges.

This is a place that your Dad (and maybe even your Mom) would like. The regular crowd includes many retirees, but has a sprinkling of construction workers, university professors, and golfers from the links next door. But it is not unusual to see a crowd with an average age of 65 or 70. The Village Bar is at its peak from late morning to early evening, with a hectic lunch bustle from 11:30 A.M. to 1 P.M. on weekdays. Casual visitors are advised drop in around 1:30 P.M. A low-keyed but sociable crowd inhabits the joint straight through the afternoon so you won't get lonesome.

The beer selection is not huge, but does fairly represent the big guys, the regionals, and micros that make Wisconsin famous. Taps usually include a Berghoff or two. Bottles round out the selection of most of southern Wisconsin's other brews. Burgers represent the main fare and are downed in great numbers.

The Village's burger is at the center of Madison's great burger dispute. For many years it was alleged that the Village had the best tavern burger in town. I remember another tavern owner responding to my query about the lack of a hamburger on his grub list with a tart "what could I do with a burger that the Village hasn't done?" That, of course, was in the days before the larding on of such exotics as sun-dried tomatoes, alfalfa sprouts, and mango preserves. I contend that the Village version is still a serviceable product suited to its station, though not up the expectations of those who nibble on their burgers in art deco juice bars surrounded by tropical plants.

▼ ▼ ▼ ▼ ▼ ▼ ▼ ▼ ▼ ▼ ▼ ▼ ▼ ▼ ▼ ▼ ▼ ▼

Madison

Wonders Pub
1980 Atwood Avenue
(608) 244-8563

More than one wag has called Wonders the Pinckney Street Hideaway Revisited after the dearly departed Capitol Square institution. That view does the Atwood Avenue spot a disservice. It's true that Wonders management gained their spurs at Pinckney Street and that many of the core customers migrated to this East Side location. But this is more of a neighborhood bar, doing without the preening of state bureaucrats, the braying of politicians, the smug smirks of lobbyists, and the intrigues of political junkies. Thank goodness!

Wonders also has a more steady day than its deceased downtown stepparent. The flow is consistent into the evening, not just lunchtime and after-work frenzies followed by flight back to the 'burbs. The atmosphere is as laid-back as you'll find in Madison. No trendy crowds looking to see who's looking at them. No gimmicks, no political correctness, and no cliques staking out turf. Just some good beers and decent tavern food and a nice mellow crowd of stand-up folks. It is a fitting stop for out-of-town visitors who want to avoid State Street madness and want something more like home.

A geniune family feeling pervades the regulars in this spot. Quite a few are related by blood or marriage, but even more have the bonds of years of frequenting the same taverns. They just don't drink together, they play together. It's quite common to see groups of Wonders patrons catching a Badger hockey game together or taking in a few innings of minor league baseball with the Madison Black Wolf.

The beer selection does well by Wisconsin specialties. Micros and regionals are in the draft mix, with Guinness for the holdovers from Pinckney Street. More imports are tallied in the bottle coolers. Wonders garners one of the best compliments a tavern can pick up: Stu Becker, former Pinckney Street co-owner, likes to drink here. Good enough for the rest of us.

Manitowoc

Capone's Pub and Grill
1036 S. 10th Street
(920) 683-8888

Despite a mild gangster motif, there's nothing sinister about this name-sake of the famous Chicago crime boss. Capone's is a favorite with the 30-something crowd, especially at night. The daytime and early-evening crowd is more age diverse, as evidenced by a wide jukebox selection that includes Benny Goodman, Patsy Cline, Jethro Tull, and Blues Traveler.

The 15 taps include Wisconsin's regionals and occasionally an import or two. Capone's switches draft beers to keep up with market developments and consumer preferences. The same sense of experimentation guides their bottled beer selection. At least 25 bottled brews are typically available, including rare finds like Beartooth Blueberry and Riverfest Stein.

Don't be surprised if a Saturday visit puts you in the middle of an informal wedding party. This seems to be the place where young folks go—after the kids and old folks polish off the wedding cake and punch—to loosen ties, take off jackets, and cast aside veils and bouquets. It's a great environment in which to get to know Manitowoc. It's not hard to find someone who will cheerfully give you the who's who of the area and stretch their information back three or four generations. I don't think that Manitowocians are particularly history minded, it's more a matter of the town having so many interwoven family stories. Family still is at the core of life in this fair city, even among these younger folks who frequent Capone's.

With this crowd, you won't hear as many working-class tales of railroading, shipbuilding, and brewing as their fathers and grandfathers might tell. But you will hear a strong work ethic that resonates in a surprising way. I didn't hear any Generation X whining or too-cool cynicism here. Hey, the kids are all right.

Food includes a sandwich menu, appetizers, and salads. Locals seem to favor the Capone Pasta Bowl and the Three Alarm Chili. Yes, it's hot. What's going on in Manitowoc taverns with the incendiary seasonings? Everywhere I went I had people asking me if I needed more hot sauce, more chilis, more salsa, and more horseradish. You can figure on drinking more than one beer to put out the flames.

▼ ▼ ▼ ▼ ▼ ▼ ▼ ▼ ▼ ▼ ▼ ▼ ▼ ▼ ▼ ▼ ▼ ▼

Manitowoc
Courthouse Pub
1001 S. 8th Street
(920) 686-1166
www.courthousepub.com

Live, fresh beer is back in this fine old brewery city that once boasted Kingsbury and others. This time it's in the form of a brewpub and restaurant in a time-honored imbibing location that some claim has been a tavern site since Honest Abe's visits to Wisconsin. There is a story here to be told about the traditions of Willinger's Beer Hall at this location.

The brew lineup combines appeal to Germanic and British palates. In the initial phases some Bavarian brews, honey wheat, amber, and stout were offered. But the plan is to assess local tastes and the broader market and add a variety of brew styles as time goes on.

While relatively new, early indications are that the Courthouse Pub is a downtown hit. The brews appeal to the genetic memories of good beer and the menu has its followers, too. Office workers gave the spot the thumbs up on both counts.

When you rate a space like this that revives traditions you can expect some good conversation. I was lucky enough to run into three distinguished gents who entertained me with three fascinating areas of local lore: railroads, maritime activity, and brewing. It was a treat to hear stories about the Soo Line and the Chicago and Northern rail activities in this part of the state. It was a delight to learn of shipwrecks and eccentric lighthouse keepers. And it was pure fun to be regaled with the accounts of the long gone Bleser and Rahr breweries. By the way, these landmarks are still around.

The real story reward was yet to come as these elder beersmen combined these elements in one yarn. Would you believe that a brewery bound railcar of malt once slipped off a ferry into the deep of Lake Michigan?

Middleton

The Club Tavern

1915 Branch Street

(608) 836-3773

Not a particularly novel name, but descriptive. It is a tavern and night-club and combines those elements well by maintaining two separate bar areas. Makes you wonder when some wag will come up with "Joe's Club Tavern Bar and Grill Lounge-Inn." Name aside, this spot has slowly but surely built up a reputation that reaches far beyond its hometown.

Middleton is known as a sedate bedroom community for Madison, not as a party town. But enter the Club Tavern and you might think you're in downtown La Crosse, or on Milwaukee's Water Street, or grooving on Madison's East Side. Over a period of years, the Club Tavern has managed to accomplish a Madison-area cultural feat: drawing Madison East Siders out of their neighborhoods for a crosstown trip. The music makes this nightspot special: heavy on blues, with dashes of rock and jazz. The live acts keep the joint jumping three and four nights a week. And "home base" status for the Westside Andy/Mel Ford Band pays dividends with a Thursday night blues jam that is more fun than big-name out-of-town acts. Even regulars never tire of that point in the second set when Mel Ford does a number with his guitar behind his back and another where the "licks" are quite literal and his tongue comes into play.

The scene here is a mixture of a number of elements, not the least of which is the warm-weather volleyball league that plays on the deep sand courts just out the back door. On some game nights the volleyball crowd is so numerous as to make it difficult to park nearby, much less get in the door. The games typically end before bands start playing, but there is sometimes a brief overlap during which sweaty coed teams share brewskis with a polo-shirt crowd.

The bands, particularly on jam nights, prompt a good measure of dancing. While the majority of patrons seem to arrive as couples or mixed groups, the regulars are fairly open to dancing with the new arrivals. Based on overheard chatter, it is easy to conclude that potential partners are usually ready, willing, and able to take a turn on the floor. Some of these folks are pretty polished, as I discovered when a woman half my size asked me to dance and proceeded to spin me around without causing grave bodily harm to anyone. Give it a whirl while the old joints can still take the punishment!

Rotated tap selections are very micro- and regional-friendly. Remember, you're just about in hops-smelling distance of the Capital Brewery/Garten Brau facility. The Club Tavern always seems to have the brand-spanking-new seasonal Garten Brau that no one else has on tap. A busy bartender told me they have "30 or 40" bottled beers.

▼ ▼ ▼ ▼ ▼ ▼ ▼ ▼ ▼ ▼ ▼ ▼ ▼ ▼ ▼ ▼ ▼

Milwaukee

Buck Bradley's Saloon and Eatery
1019 Old World Third Street
(414) 224-8500

"Impressive" is the word most often used by first-time visitors to describe the physical setting at Buck Bradley's. There are three separate bar areas, including a second-floor sports bar. The owners claim that the downstairs bar is the longest bar east of the Mississippi. The boast cannot be substantiated, but it's clear that 50 to 60 people could easily drink along its expanse without too much difficulty. The entire atmosphere is one of spaciousness and comfort.

While you're not likely to run into customers in flannel shirts and earflapped hats, there is a democratic demographic at work here. Conversation with a cross section turned up young steamfitters, middle-aged bankers, a clutch of airline flight attendants, and multigenerational family gatherings. The spot draws pretty evenly from the city, the suburbs, and the downtown convention hotels. Surprising as it may sound in 1999, Buck Bradley's serves as an initiation spot for many folks who are not part of the microbrew and brew pub subculture. So the important role of slaking thirst and whetting curiosity is performed handsomely here.

Buck Bradley's is just a buzzer-shot throw away from the Bradley Center. Staff and management prepare for event nights as if for a friendly invasion, with a special light meal and appetizer menu for the big crowds. But truth be known, crowds can be sizable on routine weekend nights. As noted already, the customers are diverse. They are also in fine form when downtown events are cooking. No problem here when it comes to eliciting a review on a nearby live concert or reliving a basketball game play-by-play.

You can find more extensive beer lists in Milwaukee. Restaurant critics cite other spots for steaks. And a number of traditional music venues might shine brighter in the entertainment department (though don't underestimate Buck Bradley's; some class local contemporary acts hold forth here on occasion). But more than one young couple told me this was their favorite spot for an evening out after a game. It's easy to see that Buck Bradley's combines many elements with flair and aplomb. Those who desire amenities with their brew won't be disappointed.

▼ ▼ ▼ ▼ ▼ ▼ ▼ ▼ ▼ ▼ ▼ ▼ ▼ ▼ ▼ ▼ ▼ ▼

Milwaukee

Derry's Pub
54 th Street and Bluemound Road
(414) 453-6008

The place for the wearing of the green year-round. If the fast-moving pints of Guinness and Harp fail to give away the ethnic leanings of the proprietor, the several versions of the Hegarty family crest and the wall map of Ireland will set you straight. But you don't have to be Irish to be welcome here. The regulars include a fair number of O'Schmidts, O'Cohens, and O'Lewandowskis. Many of my urban tavern buddies swear that Derry's is one of Milwaukee's best connections with its salad days as machine shop to the world.

Part neighborhood pub, part political hangout, and part sports bar, Derry's draws a diverse crowd that includes county officials and die-hard Milwaukee Brewers fans. Indeed, in late spring the bar chatter is more likely to be focused on the Cub's latest losing streak than NBA and NHL playoffs. Derry's anchors a strip of bars, cafes, and sports memorabilia shops across the street from the strange structure at the gate of Cavalry Cemetery.

The talk often runs political, though not of the refined theoretical kind. In Derry's it can range from the "troubles" of Northern Ireland to the rough and tumble of big city ward politics to the old progressive labor variety that dominated the city for much of the first half of this century. Though in recent years there's been a merger of sports talk and political banter in these quarters as passions engage on stadium construction, the business acumen of sports franchise owners, and the future of the Brewers.

There are few places in Milwaukee that stay as busy from lunch to bar time. It's an ideal place to go for lunch before a Brewers' day game. Alone you can squeeze in at the bar. With a small group you can occupy a comfortable booth. Or if you've brought a busload you can arrange for the use of the banquet room. You can walk to the stadium, come back for a beer after the game and let the traffic get out of town.

It should be noted that the surrounding blocks have the makings of a decent pub crawl, including a number of modern sportsbars. The whole neighborhood is absolutely bonkers on Brewers opening days. Though there is much to prize about Milwaukee as a big small town, the opening days in these few square blocks puts humble Wisconsinites smack dab in line with all the storied neighborhoods around all the past and present major league parks.

▼ ▼ ▼ ▼ ▼ ▼ ▼ ▼ ▼ ▼ ▼ ▼ ▼ ▼ ▼ ▼ ▼ ▼

Milwaukee
Foundation
2718 Bremen Street
(414) 374-2587

T hough they've redecorated and scaled back the skateboard collection, this still remains one of Wisconsin's quirkier joints. You can still expect to run into a party here that includes some colorful people or some entourage or other that just blew in from points unknown. Or it just might hit at a time when Milwaukee's guerrilla homebrewers are hosting a tasting party. Foundation is also a hangout for a number of musicians and band hangers-on. At least one Milwaukee source *(The Shepherd Express)* gave the bar's jukebox the top rating in the Milwaukee area.

And talk about characters! Each story that filters back to me about this place is stranger than the last. My own foray exposed me to a couple who spoke to each other in dialogue lines lifted from the Rocky Horror Picture Show, a juggler with about a dozen body piercings, and a woman who told me she was practicing to be a female impersonator. Were they pulling my leg or other body parts? All I know is that I came away feeling like it was audience participation night at a punk version of public radio's Hotel Milwaukee show. But the strangest thing of all is that everyone was as nice as a small town homecoming.

Tavern owners seldom recognize how important it is for the establishment to have a personality. It doesn't matter if the ambience is mounted mythological beasts or vehicle license plates. We need more bars with distinctive character. So hats off to this one!

They usually offer eight to ten tap beers. Local brews are well represented, including Sprecher and Lakefront products. The folks across the pond are acknowledged with Guinness and Hacker-Pschorr. This is not a snooty microbrew bar. They are not embarrassed by their sales volume of Blatz (sold at $1 per) nor their unpretentious setting. At Foundation they keep one foot firmly planted in Milwaukee's 1950's tavern tradition and one foot boldly stepping into the 21st Century. They pull it off.

▼　▼　▼　▼　▼　▼　▼　▼　▼　▼　▼　▼　▼　▼　▼　▼　▼

Milwaukee

Hampton House
5403 West Hampton Avenue
(414) 461-2108

A neighborhood bar is usually the last place you expect to find diversity. In many places, the neighborhood bar is still a reflection of the ethnic identity or socioeconomic class of the predominant group in surrounding residential areas. But here, in one of America's most segregated cities, we have in Hampton House a long-standing tradition of African-American and European-American customer mingling.

The atmosphere is friendly, not forced, and reflects the positive side of social changes in Milwaukee over the last few decades. In some cases the friendships span several generations. Fathers may have worked in the machine shop together and daughters may have attended UW-Milwaukee together. Not surprisingly, it is a comfortable spot for those with multiracial backgrounds. That is a growing portion of the population, and eventually smart businesspeople will figure out it's a niche market.

This establishment carves its own tranquil spot in the complex business of creating community in a diverse environment. Candid talk with customers disabuses one of any utopian fantasies. Different people getting along in the hustle and bustle of competitive urban life will always be a challenge. What is heartening about people I met here is how unassuming and honest they are about their responsibility for building that new world that most of us want.

This is one of the few places in Wisconsin where I have run into people who still talk about the unfinished business of civil rights, not the language of intergroup grievances. If you build some trust in this circle you just might get a person or two to open up about the long, hot summers of the past and the stories and humor of cultural misunderstandings.

Not a micro bar, but there are some hometown and regional beers to be had. The big pastime is dart throwing. The restaurant portion of the business also has a neighborhood following.

▼ ▼ ▼ ▼ ▼ ▼ ▼ ▼ ▼ ▼ ▼ ▼ ▼ ▼ ▼ ▼ ▼

Milwaukee
Landmark 1850 Inn
5905 S. Howell Avenue
(414) 769-1850

Milwaukee's oldest tavern! What more need be said about a history-steeped spot that hosted rebellious Whigs planning the formation of the Republican Party and free soil vigilantes fresh off a mission to liberate a fugitive slave? What more could be remarked on its classic building form, which is only two years shy of the age of the state of Wisconsin? What praise could be uttered about hospitality practices that are already praised to the heights by magazine writers and beer fanciers?

Well, one could say that the Landmark 1850 Inn is in the heart of south side Milwaukee. One could praise a kitchen open seven evenings a week (this is a night spot, kitchen hours 3pm to closing). One could give thanks for published coupons conferring complimentary and discounted goodies upon customers. And one could find fellowship with the other patrons of this fair inn.

The spot does draw some history buffs, but I found far more patrons who are quietly making history. The Landmark 1850 Inn seems to be a favorite among those who do their share of downtown lunches and have their fill of being seen at same. The ones I run into are usually involved with business associations, nonprofit organizations, educational groups, and fraternal orders. So I get the sense that a fair amount of networking goes on here.

It also seems to be a place where people open up about what makes Milwaukee tick. This city of beer and sausage is not a terribly introspective place and it is often hard to get answers about the inner workings of civic life. Sometimes it seems like the formal structure of the community is just an illusion and the real shots are being called elsewhere. The patrons at the Landmark 1850 Inn have often shared astute observations with me about the intrigues surrounding Milwaukee's world of finance and development. Oddly enough, many of the tales lead back to the great brewing fortunes. You can get lost in those plot lines.

But don't forget the beer. The selections can vary from time to time, but are always rich and diverse. Among the recent treats: three lambics, a trappist ale, and a Norwegian brew.

▼ ▼ ▼ ▼ ▼ ▼ ▼ ▼ ▼ ▼ ▼ ▼ ▼ ▼ ▼ ▼ ▼ ▼ ▼

Milwaukee

Landmark Lanes
2220 N. Farwell Avenue
(414) 278-8770

Landmark Lanes has been sniped at in Milwaukee's newspapers and magazines as the place to go for a walk on the dark side. The place is panned by suburban entertainment writers for its funky crowd and late-night drink specials. But those folks like the bright lights. Have they no appreciation for the real heartbeat of the city?

It's true Landmark Lanes has a notes-from-the-underground feel. But many of us interpret its atmosphere as a deft combination of bowling alley and undercover agent rendezvous site. More than a few public defenders, detectives, and investigative writers have mentioned this spot as a place where information can be found and the tip of the unseen Milwaukee can be glimpsed. Folklore has it that the principals of a famous espionage case dallied here and that labor union and political power struggles have been settled here by incognito insiders. Never fear, intrigue does not translate into sinister surroundings—the spot is safe if you apply urban common sense.

Some of my favorite Milwaukee barroom buds like to hang out here. They're honest about liking the atmosphere as much as the beer. It is a place where stories can run as light and cheery as a fine pilsner or as dark and heavy as a coffee stout. Many of my favorite tale spinners in this joint come down somewhere between the conflicted tales of morally ambiguous postindustrial life and the blunt sensationalism of true-crime tabloids. On the other hand, I know of no other place in Milwaukee where a ribald story resonates quite so well. All through the various narrations there is the endless sipping.

How about that beer? First-time visitors are surprised to find 39 tap lines and 75 types of bottled beer. The selections balance the giants, the micros, the regionals, and the imports. Put on your trenchcoat or leather jacket and don your sunglasses.

▼ ▼ ▼ ▼ ▼ ▼ ▼ ▼ ▼ ▼ ▼ ▼ ▼ ▼ ▼ ▼ ▼ ▼

Milwaukee

La Perla
734 S. Fifth Street
(414) 645-9888

A Friday night hotspot in a noted Mexican-American restaurant on Milwaukee's South Side. The lively crowd mixes plenty of Spanish and Spanish accents with German-American and Polish-American customers. The mood is more samba and Latin disco than mariachi. As one regular put it, "It's a good place to go if you can't get away to Puerto Vallarta." To that claim my response is it's better in food and hospitality, lacking only the warm and sunny weather that drives one south of the border in winter.

La Perla serves the full range of tropical drinks, with blender concoctions being very popular. If there's a bigger tequila selection in Wisconsin, I haven't seen it. The primary Mexican beers are available (Modela, Negra Modelo, Carta Blanca, Pacifico, Dos Equis, Dos Equis Lager Bohemia, and Corona) along with other domestics and imports. No simple cantina, La Perla's bar is among the classiest spots in Milwaukee to imbibe your favorite beverage.

All 50-plus restaurant menu items can be ordered in the bar. It's clear that many of the regular customers routinely take their meals in the bar. The *botanas* (appetizers) and combination plates seem to be the main barroom fare. But as I sipped my Dos Equis and nibbled fresh tortilla chips on my first visit, the businessman on the next stool went to work on sautéed lobster and garlic sauce.

This bright, well-lit restaurant has secure parking, which is reassuring to out-of-towners after they approach through a dimly lit warehouse district. The outside patio area is a slice of Margaritaville in summer. In the winter the deck is covered with a walled-in tent, warmed by kerosene heaters and filled with tables. This may sound a little like field manuevers with NATO or mess hall à la *M*A*S*H*, but it's quite cozy and altogether serviceable. Not to mention that it keeps down the waiting time to be seated. So bravo to La Perla management. Check out the collection of hundreds of hot sauces in the bar.

Milwaukee

Milwaukee Ale House

233 N. Water Street
(414) 226-2337
www.ale-house.com

One of Wisconsin's most acclaimed brew pubs, the Milwaukee Ale House is a hangout for those connected to the microbrewing industry. The person next to you at the bar might be a micro brewery owner, sales rep from a malt processor, or a brewery equipment engineer. But your stoolmate could just as well turn out to be "Joe from da southside." And who can blame him for wandering into the land of "da suits." The beer and the food stand out even in a town with no shortage of choices.

Yes, the beer! Let me count the ways. For the novice palate, there is the honey wheat Downtown Lite. For the hardy veteran, there is Sheepshead Stout, brimming with the rich taste of dark roasted malt. Rounding out the selections are Scotch Red, Solomon Juneau Golden Ale, and Pub Chair Pale Ale. All distinctive and worth sampling before you zero in on a favorite.

The management has wisely avoided the chauvinism that overtakes may full-line brew pubs. They are confident enough about their products (and yet solicitous of customer preferences) to offer many other Wisconsin microbrews, including the seasonals. On past visits my crew encountered wide selections of their regional favorites. They expect to offer seasonal brews from most of Wisconsin's micro breweries.

As if all this wasn't enough, the Ale House has built an impressive wine list, a decent selection of scotch, and a trove of fine cigars. Live music almost every night! The Ale House books the type of acts that bring people to their feet.

▼ ▼ ▼ ▼ ▼ ▼ ▼ ▼ ▼ ▼ ▼ ▼ ▼ ▼ ▼ ▼ ▼

Milwaukee

O'Brien's Sports Bar and Grill
N. 49th and W. Vliet Streets
(414) 453-6200

M any tavern denizens (myself included) dread change, especially when they've grown accustomed to the comfort and amenities of a time-worn watering hole. This was once the site of a novel import-beer tavern called the Golden Zither. But that was many bottles ago, and in this case the past is redeemed and expanded upon. My brew scouts give the new place a hearty thumbs-up and commend the updated offerings and look.

O'Brien's logs in with 17 beer taps. The microbrew mainstays are the local products from Lakefront and Sprecher. The import side of the ledger tilts toward the British Isles with Newcastle, Harp, and Guinness. They plan to carry a bottle inventory of around a hundred brands. Look for $2 import night on Thursdays.

The crowd is lively and beer focused, though you find less of the beer-sampling crowd here and more customers who know what they like. The mood is decidedly different than in the downtown establishments—more of a sense of dropping by for a fitting end to the day rather than knocking back a quick drink before scooting out to the 'burbs. The neighborhood has undergone some changes but is still remembered by most as the core of Milwaukee's solid working-class families. It's kind of interesting when those who've hung on in these parts encounter the self-styled urban renewalists who are now coming back from the 'burbs. Provides some good material for the amateur sociologists among us.

Music is building up a following, too. Regulars love the visiting blues, rock, jazz, and Irish bands. The menu expanded from sandwiches into fish fry territory and pizza.

▼ ▼ ▼ ▼ ▼ ▼ ▼ ▼ ▼ ▼ ▼ ▼ ▼ ▼ ▼ ▼ ▼ ▼

Milwaukee

Thai Joe's (in the Bangkok Orchid Restaurant)
2238 N. Prospect Avenue
(414) 223-3333
www.taijoes.com

Spend part of your youth in Southeast Asia? Well then, here's a spot that might trigger some memories (and without the gecko lizards and dysentery that might accompany a visit to those youthful haunts). Although those former enlisted men among us would probably also recall that the commissioned officers had a way of keeping places this nice to themselves.

Is it too much of a bamboo curtain fantasy to wonder what secrets lurk in such a place? It seems that each time I visit Thai Joe's there's some Hollywood stock character whispering to a bartender. One time it was a heavy Sidney Greenstreet look-alike in a tropical white suit. And what about that phone number's hidden code? G.I.s of my era will recall that .223 is the English system caliber for the 5.56mm ammunition fired by the M-16 and 33 was the formaldehyde laced beer called ba moui ba in the defunct Republic of Vietnam. Coincidence? You be the judge.

Actually the Asian motif can throw you in spite of the worthy Thai restaurant associated with the site. As night descends and deepens in this neighborhood the place becomes decidedly bohemian and has hosted its share of poets and guitar-strumming folkies. Often there is live music three and four nights a week and Grateful Dead nights on Friday. The late crowds can seem equal parts punk and Warren Zevonists. So you know where to send your lawyers and money (skip the guns).

Though you might expect cocktails and tropical drinks to dominate in such club climes, beer is spoken clearly here with a respectable selection draft and bottle-wise. During the last visit by the roving tavern tourers we sampled tap Heineken, Riverwest Stein and Two-Headed Ale.

▼ ▼ ▼ ▼ ▼ ▼ ▼ ▼ ▼ ▼ ▼ ▼ ▼ ▼ ▼ ▼ ▼ ▼ ▼

Milwaukee

Turner Restaurant Bar
1034 N. Fourth Street
(414) 276-4844

No tour of Wisconsin's imbibing establishments would be complete without mention of the bar in the Historic Turner Restaurant (yes, the word "historic" is part of the formal business name). The landmark building is deeply steeped in the cultural and political traditions of Wisconsin's German community. Turner *Verein*, or clubs, once dotted the landscape and served as athletic clubs for Wisconsin's largest ethnic group. The Milwaukee association kept this building in good repair and offered good food and drink to five generations of German Americans.

Perhaps more importantly, the continuation of the Turner club established a link with Milwaukee's golden age. It was a time not of an ethnic minority in an American city, but of a German city in the American heartland. This meant lectures, concerts, choral societies, newspapers, publishing houses, and all manner of learned professions carried out within a central European worldview. The leisurely Sunday spent in parks with the family and a bucket of beer was no small part of this milieu and accounted for the bitter resistance in Milwaukee toward the Prohibition movement. Turner Hall is seen by many as a monument to those times.

Then came the renovations of the last decade. Many of the regulars think the changes swept away the worn beer hall charm that provided their Friday night sanctuary. But the murals, artifacts, and photograph collection remain. So do the traditional elements of the menu. If anything, the fish fry and sandwiches are better than ever. Indeed, many younger folks are returning to the place Grandpa took them to years ago. It is a great piece in the downtown refurbishing puzzle.

As for the beer, there is a growing emphasis on the local microbrews, and the import collection is up to about two dozen Teutonic favorites. The bar setting is virtually a gilded palace. Besides the bar and an elegant dining area, there are also party and meeting rooms that are suitable for large group entertaining.

Milwaukee

Water Street Brewery

1101 N. Water Street
(414) 272-1195
www.waterstreetbrewery.com/wsb

Back in 1987 it seemed like a bold proposition to combine a small brewery and restaurant. Since then they're springing up all over the place. But, despite many excellent additions to the downtown Milwaukee scene, loyal patrons cast their votes for this trailblazer. Water Street shows no sign of letting up or running out of steam.

It would be difficult to catalogue the range of brews to come out of Water Street kettles over the years. Never adverse to experimentation, they still punch out novel seasonal beers in addition to regular house brews. Our crew sampled honey lager, pale ale, doppelbock, amber, weiss, and oktoberfest and pronounced them "sehr gut." I was very partial to the oktoberfest. I hauled a growler of it home to Iowa County. Water Street efforts have not gone unnoticed in brewing trade publications.

Lunch is offered in the form of appetizers, sandwiches, and salads. A dinner menu comes into play in the evening hours. Self-aware as an "institution," Water Street Brewery offers tours and souvenir sales. Growing numbers of out of town visitors are learning that no trip to Milwaukee is complete without a visit to Water Street. Their updated website is one of the best I've seen in terms of keeping the customer posted. It has a cute color display of the various beers and a good basic explanation of the beermaking process.

As the prior Milwaukee entries show there are places aplenty where beerlovers congregate to savor beer, appreciate beer, and even venerate beer. Water Street draws on all those responses and adds a few that it has earned by virtue of its seniority. The one element that they preserve that is often forgotten in the serious brewpub is pure fun. There is more laughter here than any other similar operation.

It's no accident that the groups that meet to celebrate brewing history, swap homebrew recipes, and plan beer festival events often pick Water Street as the place to hatch their plots or kick off their efforts. The atmosphere is contagious. Stop in and kick off a little beer adventure of your own.

ANOTHER ROUND

Some Milwaukee Beer Facts

Beer made Milwaukee famous because of location, resources, and immigration patterns. Milwaukee sat astride the new rail routes. It had ready access to grain for brewing and wood for barrels. The waves of German immigrants brought brewing experience and consumer demand.

Miller's flagship brew, High Life, was named in a 1906 contest. The logo for many years was the "Girl in the Moon," who in various depictions wore a witchlike hat and wielded a whip. Miller diverted its production during World War II to our troops overseas and built up a national following.

Pabst Brewing Company was one of the first breweries to understand the marketing potential of awards. It actively promoted the beer at nineteenth-century fairs and expositions. Pabst beer garnered honors at the 1876 Philadelphia Centennial Exposition, the 1878 Paris World's Fair, and the 1893 Columbia Exposition in Chicago. In 1892 the company used 300,000 yards of blue ribbon, a snip of which was wrapped around the neck of each bottle of its premium beer. After World War II, Pabst evolved into a working-class favorite. By the 1990s closure of the Milwaukee facilities and cuts in benefits for retired brewery workers had made the name a dirty word in union halls.

▼ ▼ ▼ ▼ ▼ ▼ ▼ ▼ ▼ ▼ ▼ ▼ ▼ ▼ ▼ ▼ ▼ ▼ ▼

Mount Horeb

Grumpy Troll Brew Pub
105 S. 2nd Street
(608) 437-2739

Resurrection and reincarnation are interesting notions, but they don't always translate well to taverns and brewpubs. You've seen the syndrome; a favorite old spot goes down for the count and upon resuscitation in other hands it just doesn't quite capture its former glory or allure. It's just the opposite here, the Grumpy Troll builds upon the former Mount Horeb Brew Pub's foundation and does some things better.

For starters, the physical layout is much improved. It's more comfy and pleasing to the eye. The acoustic echo bounce has also been dialed down. The staff is more on the ball as well. Now it's a spot where you can get downright comfortable at the bar.

The real reason to go into the place is the beer. The patron troll spirits of Mount Horeb must add something to the fermentation process, since I've enjoyed everything that gets brewed in this town. Here's the latest lineup: Grumpy Stout, Red-Eyed Troll, How-Now Brown Cow, Trailside Wheat, Troll's Gold Lager, Winter Warmer Ale, Bitter Troll and Rye Bock. Evocative names and enjoyable brews that fit almost every mood and taste. I am especially partial to the Rye Bock and recommend to those ready to move beyond the "air bread" versions of beer.

The menu is extensive enough to cover your bases for lunch and dinner. The locals like the Black Angus burgers. I've had good experiences with the soups.

Note that there's a ton of stuff to do right in Mount Horeb and a fair amount of sightseeing and recreation in the vicinity. This is a boon to the casual tavern visitor. The rigorous devotee will like the town because he can ditch his tourist companion and cruise Mount Horeb's quirky little bars, visit the solid Main Street Pub and Grill, hit the brewpub a second time, and still make it into Prairie Books so that you can fool those picking you up into thinking you browsed the stacks all afternoon. Hey, it works for me.

Also, since you're this close, you might as well visit Hooterville Inn in Blue Mounds. It's only a few miles to the west.

▼ ▼ ▼ ▼ ▼ ▼ ▼ ▼ ▼ ▼ ▼ ▼ ▼ ▼ ▼ ▼ ▼ ▼

Oshkosh
Packers Pub
1603 West 20th Avenue
(920) 231-3517

Guess what interest tops the list at this spot? Actually, gridiron passion is only part of the story. While Packer hearts may beat beneath their green and gold attire, patrons here make the place lively throughout all four seasons. Next door is La Sures Cafe and Catering, and together the two businesses make this stretch of 20th Avenue just about the busiest block in Winnebago County on Friday night. Packers Pub is proof that the bustle of the neighborhood tavern can be carried out to the edge of a city as it changes through growth. The trick is meshing with the new patterns of housing and business development and, unfortunately, conceding that almost all patrons will arrive by car. That slam at Fox Valley land use aside, Packers Pub does the after-work tavern tradition proud.

Speaking of Friday night, arrive before the after-work crowd starts filing in—it often ends up four deep at the bar. So what's the draw? The menu is not extensive, though they make a darn good chicken salad sandwich. The average customer might think of Coors as a premium beer, but press a bit and they'll admit they've heard of Leinenkugel.

It probably comes down to nice people having a good time in a comfortable setting. There's a fairly even gender distribution here among this sports-inclined, but not couch potato, crowd. These are not just spectators—there are plenty of golfers, softball players, and winter-sports enthusiasts here, both male and female.

Packers Pub runs on a seasonal cycle not too different from that of many Wisconsin taverns: football season at the center, various sports playoffs following, and the rear brought up by a variety of special events in the family calendar like anniversaries, birthdays, and graduations. If you happen to be in the area on a Packer road game day, this is definitely the place to watch the game.

Another interesting local phenomenon occurs during the summer when the annual aviation event hits town. All manner of pilots, jet junkies, military aircraft buffs, and aerospace business types descend on Oshkosh and take this and virtually every other bar over for the duration. It's a great time if you like aircraft and don't mind humongous crowds. I sat in Packers Pub on one occasion and heard crop dusters, stunt pilots, and airline executives trade insults with World War II bomber pilots. I'll always remember Packers Pub as the place where I finally met the Navy pilot who nearly bombed me in Vietnam 30 years ago. Apology and round of beer accepted.

▼ ▼ ▼ ▼ ▼ ▼ ▼ ▼ ▼ ▼ ▼ ▼ ▼ ▼ ▼ ▼ ▼ ▼ ▼

Oshkosh

Peabody's Ale House
544 N. Main Street
(608) 235-4004

Boy, do I owe the folks at Peabody's Ale House an apology. They were supposed to be in the first edition of the tavern guide and I goofed it up. Somehow I managed to craft a mutant entry that partially described Peabody's and grafted it on to an entry on Oblio's, another fine Main Street establishment. It was a good year before I could show my face again in downtown Oshkosh.

You're probably thinking, here's a guy who goes into hundreds of taverns and samples their wares. You might allow that the rigors of such field research might introduce an error or two into the resulting text. But the slight to Peabody's (and Oblio's) is worse than that. My notes on my Oshkosh trips were, let us say, imbued with late evening ambiguity. So I consulted other sources who must have had their own ambiguities to deal with. The result: a guidebook entry that no one conversant with Oshkosh could make head or tail of.

This time I took compass and topographical map and will attest that the premises described lovingly below are indeed Peabody's as encountered without benefit of prior stops. It's certainly worthy of being your first stop in Oshkosh. They boast 17 taps, hefty with imports and micros. On my GPS-coordinated visit, Hinterland Pale Ale was the hot item. Another plus: eight single malts for those with a taste for the strong stuff.

Peabody's Ale House has a great sandwich menu. My buddies like the Rueben and turkey sub. Among the regulars the pizzas seemed to garner favor. One fellow piped up on behalf of the gyros.

The evening crowd seemed to run toward the twenty-somethings and thirty-somethings. But we found them tolerant of duffers. Whilst in downtown Oshkosh saunter down to 434 Main Street and try Oblio's, also worth a visit.

▼ ▼ ▼ ▼ ▼ ▼ ▼ ▼ ▼ ▼ ▼ ▼ ▼ ▼ ▼ ▼ ▼ ▼

Poynette

Hookers Resort
Highway V at Lake Wisconsin
(608) 635-7867

Hookers has earned the loyalty of three and four generations within the families that frequent the east bank of the Lake Wisconsin section of the Wisconsin River. Even those who didn't spend their childhoods here will feel the connection to those family-friendly lakeside taverns of 40 and 50 years ago. These are very precious pieces of the cultural landscape and are threatened by trends in the use of shoreline property that act to price small businesses out of such spots and give them over to playgrounds and retreats for the well-off. It's a touchy matter that agitates the nerves connected to our populist sensibilities and to our conservationist values.

Older patrons can fill you in about their memories of polkas and square dances. There was a time when the Poynette radio station would plug the performances by having the musicians give live on-air samples. Many a big name passed through Columbia County courtesy of this process. These days the bands present contemporary country and oldies rock on Friday and Saturday nights. Wednesdays bring line dancing and Sundays often bring jam sessions. Schedules can vary due to reserved evenings for wedding parties and reunions, so call ahead.

The bar is not fancy but has a loyal following. The 30 bottled brews do not include many exotics, being anchored chiefly by the big guys in Milwaukee and St. Louis. However, effort is made to keep the complete Leinie's craft line on hand. Morning-after visitors will also appreciate the good-sized Bloody Mary served with full-size pickle and beefstick.

The Hookers bar menu is limited to sandwiches and deep-fried appetizers. If you saunter over to the dining room you can rustle up steaks and fish, including perch, cod, walleye, and the rarely seen bluegill. The resort side of the business is a bit of "up north" without the long drive. Cabins are available. Good fishing can be found on the river and at nearby Columbia Lake. The adjacent marina provides canoe rentals, excursions, and return transport.

If you're up for conversation at Hookers, catch a Saturday afternoon crowd on a winter day after a cold spell that has created mass cabin fever. This is when the area's true brandy sippers crawl out to see their shadows and limber up their tales of ice fishing, snow softball, snow golf, and the gentlemen's ice sport of curling. Or show up some Friday night near the time of the summer solstice, when the purple rays of the fading sunset darn near bump up against evening news time. These are the dog days of fishermen's lies, comic boat mishaps, and encounters with DNR conservation wardens. Either way you're likely to run into a Gunderson who'll work in a Norwegian joke.

39

▼ ▼ ▼ ▼ ▼ ▼ ▼ ▼ ▼ ▼ ▼ ▼ ▼ ▼ ▼ ▼ ▼ ▼ ▼

Racine

Swingers
2322 Lathrop Avenue
(262) 554-0880

A visit to Swingers is not a visit to the Racine that many of us knew in the days of bustling machine shops and heavy equipment manufacturing. It is becoming harder and harder to find traces of that Racine. In a sense, a spot like Swingers is emblematic of the shift in economic base that many of Wisconsin's midrange cities were forced to muddle through. Though one can hear nostalgic laments for many lost shot-and-a-beer joints, there is a clear understanding that the customer base has changed and that many of the enduring bars now offer more customer options.

The six-tap rotation at Swingers is usually anchored by Hacker-Pschorr and Rolling Rock, with guest appearances by Sprecher and Gray's products. The bottled list tallies around 25 to 30 brands from among the big-name imports, domestic nationals, and a few micros. Inexplicably, pumpkin ale has followers here beyond the seasonal demand at Halloween and Thanksgiving. Many regulars come for the daily drink specials, and many women customers like the hot nut-honey drink.

Swingers adopts that all-things-to-all-people approach taken by T.G.I. Friday's and other chains. That's not a put-down; it's good to see an independent adapt to wide-band consumer demand. One senses that the appeal here represents a generational changing of the tavern guard. The old after-work tavern was often a totally male domain. In those days, when a man went out with the wife for a drink in Racine, he put on a coat and a tie. Nowadays, the prime age base of taverngoers in places like Racine is looking for a middle ground, and Swingers provides it. The atmosphere is casual but the food is many notches above that.

One of my favorite things about the crowd at Swingers is that they're young enough to move on to the next phase of tavern life, but old enough to have an appreciation for what has been lost in the neighborhoods of Racine and places like Kenosha, Cudahy, South Milwaukee, and West Allis. A few even played a little game of Dad's/Granddad's favorite bar. The way I heard it during my visit, this trivial but nostalgic pursuit was consciously part homage and part send-up. How else can you explain the sentimental tears shed at the loss of the forebears' manly haunts along with the guffaws over the urinals that backed up during the celebrations marking the end of World War II and stayed clogged until the day the business died?

▼ ▼ ▼ ▼ ▼ ▼ ▼ ▼ ▼ ▼ ▼ ▼ ▼ ▼ ▼ ▼ ▼ ▼ ▼

Racine

Yardarm Bar and Grill

930 Erie Street
(262) 633-8270

The nautical crew ties up here in weather fair and foul. The atmosphere is, naturally, driven by the maritime theme and includes artifacts from vessels such as Aristotle Onassis's mega yacht and Lake Michigan shipwrecks. But don't expect boating snobbery here—the putt-putt skiff folks mingle with the nattily attired sailing crowd. In addition, plenty of landlubbers come on board just because a friend told them the place is seaworthy.

The Yardarm sails with ten taps of rotating selections but is often graced with the likes of Guinness, Bass, Harp, Newcastle, Rolling Rock, and Leinenkugel. The bottled selection of 20 beers runs more toward the big nationals, though Illinois boaters have created a demand for Goose Island microbrews. The two-for-one Bloody Mary special has a following among regular patrons. Crowd profile tilts quite a bit toward groups, small and large, who arrive together. But that should not deter the lone castaway from seeking refuge on these shores.

The sandwiches and seafood have a good reputation. The grilled sea bass is spoken of fondly. The Yardarm burger was, in recent memory, cited as a Wisconsin standout. Live music finds its way here on a fairly regular basis (more in summer). It's the type of place with a lot of comings and goings of transient customers. That sort of position often makes it difficult for an establishment to develop a core of regulars who are the necessary ingredient in incubating a tavern culture. But the Yardarm does indeed have its loyal locals and its repeat out-of-towners who crew the place on a sustained basis and keep it shipshape for the new passengers.

Don't expect the type of maritime conversation that you might find in Algoma, Manitowoc, or Superior. You won't find leather-skinned freighter hands in here. But you will find spillover from Racine's summertime lake events, be they sailing or fishing tournaments. Just as likely is an encounter with the movers and shakers of Racine and a dialogue on the changes that first rocked the city and then brought it back. On occasion the talk turns to the Old World Racine, which, while not as thoroughly European as Milwaukee in its heyday, had pockets of Continental charm that still echo today. A little prodding will help the locals wax eloquent on their kringle pastries from Denmark, the kitchen practices from Italy, and the fish dishes from Norway. Try as the developers might to reinvent things, this is still Wisconsin. .

Sheboygan

Dave's Who's Inn
835 Indiana Avenue
(920) 457-9832

Weekend nights may test your eardrums with heavy metal music. But, as they say, if it's too loud, you're too old for these nights (unless your favorite bands of the sixties and seventies already left you hearing impaired). Luckily the high-volume stuff is upstairs and the drinks are cheaper on the ground floor. But don't discount the possibility that you might just have some interesting exchanges with the regulars. You just need to yell a little louder.

Some observers see Dave's as the best young blue-collar bar between Milwaukee and Green Bay. The label is a bit deceptive since you're likely to see some gray beards come in for the food and game area. It has its own following for its Friday night perch plate, and broasted chicken is served throughout the week. It's this crowd that has the widest range and the most offbeat characters. But they like to chow down together. Regulars say it's the best place in town for a pickup game of darts or pool (four tables).

Dave's is also home to an odd custom of washing down chicken wings with large quantities of Foster's draft lager. The Australian brew is used as a chaser for regular, hot, or nuclear versions of the poultry appendage. No one could tell me how the tradition started, and as far as anyone knew there was no local link to Down Under.

My roving band of merry men did find a traveling subculture here that has made forays as far as Sun Prairie, if not Sydney. Some of the young fellows who frequent this spot work in construction and installation trades. We heard about road building, electronic cable laying, and pipeline construction. So our group of middle-aged guys received a lesson in where the metal crowd hangs out these days, where the hot after-hours raves go down, and where young laborers get their tattoos. We also found a tradition among some of Dave's patrons that involves celebration of seasonal layoffs and departure for sunnier climes. This is a new spin to the old building trades custom of using winter for hunting, ice fishing, and tavern hopping. Come that January subzero blast, you can't blame them.

▼ ▼ ▼ ▼ ▼ ▼ ▼ ▼ ▼ ▼ ▼ ▼ ▼ ▼ ▼ ▼ ▼ ▼

Sheboygan
Ziggy's Bar and Grill
933 Indiana Avenue
(920) 457-3325

Family-style taverns have fallen somewhat out of style as soccer moms and dads must spend more time chauffeuring Ryan and Brittany to activities and less time socializing with aunts, uncles, and neighbors. In Sheboygan, the tradition is kept alive with Ziggy's Saturday-afternoon brat fries, junior brass bands, and dart tournaments. The result is a cordial tavern where advice, directions, and gossip are readily dispensed along with the beer.

It also acts as a statement that this straight-arrow portion of the Sheboyganese, exemplary work habits aside, understand the need to slow down the pace. It is unusual to find a cluster of folks like this who openly repudiate the money chase in favor of spending time with family and friends. One old sage remarked that the hurried pace of life these days has done more to harm tavern fellowship than drinking age changes, traffic safety concerns, and competing entertainment options. The end of the workday once offered the promise of unwinding time. Now it's errand time. Ziggy's seems to understand that and fights against the trend.

Ziggy's is a no-frills, country tavern in the city. Patrons come back often for chicken-to-go orders, and the practice is catching on with travelers and fishing parties. Loyalists claim this home turf as the lakeshore's most rabid Packerbacker bar. There are those from Port Washington to Two Rivers who would dispute that, but this crowd is definitely in the running. What is beyond dispute is the sociable nature of the people on both sides of the bar. A vehicle problem in our party of pub pilgrims was met by a four-person volunteer crew out of Ziggy's, including one who went home for tools to effect the needed repair.

The Good Samaritan episode presented another rare slice of life when one up-in-years sidewalk supervisor came out to educate us about road etiquette in the Depression era. He related some interesting stories about a code of the road that evolved as more people had access to automobiles and roved the newly paved highways. He made it sound like every breakdown was a social occasion as other motorists stopped to assist and nearby farmers brought out cool water. And he claimed, with a wink of the eye, that the helpee owed the helpers a drink the next time they met in a tavern. Never let it be said that we didn't repay our obligation.

The beer selection is not extensive, but it does include bottled Point and Leinie's. We cheerfully bought a half dozen Points for our volunteer mechanics. Anheuser-Busch craft brews are available on tap, and they were still in fine form during our visit. Private parties often fill the dining area, so you can expect to have your perch sandwich and beer at the bar with the regulars.

43

▼ ▼ ▼ ▼ ▼ ▼ ▼ ▼ ▼ ▼ ▼ ▼ ▼ ▼ ▼ ▼ ▼

ANOTHER ROUND

What's In a Tavern Name?

Many tavern owners consider the naming process one of the most important steps in starting a business. The names they choose often fuse personal identity with the business identity. Sometimes the names project an image that builds a community and attracts a desired clientele.

Tavern names run from distinguished to mundane to madcap. Among Wisconsin's 14,000-plus taverns are both diversity and recurrent themes. One-of-a-kind names are balanced by a handful of names that are repeated over and over upon the landscape.

The moniker "Sportsmen's Bar," and its variants, wins the prize for sheer numbers. You can't drive far without seeing the name. Indeed, Scott Stenger of Wisconsin's Tavern League told me that many people play a pub crawling game that credits those who find the first Sportsmen's and the most Sportsmen's.

There are numerous "Anchor Inns"—some far from water. Tavern owners make liberal use of the handle "Fireside," notwithstanding the lack of fireplaces or woodstoves. Many others incorporate their highway number in the name, as in Club 117.

On the other hand, Wisconsin taverns also sport names that reflect whimsy, cynicism, insider humor, and long nights of cheap liquor. Some record our heritage and serve as cultural benchmarks. A handful even reflect modern culture's marital instability with X'd-out spouse names still visible on signs.

Pardtown Pub of Linden is a favorite in the heritage category. The name records the original name and ambience of this 1827 Cornish settlement. The Grey Ghost of Forest Junction has a name that echoes.

My list of fun names includes: The Place To Be (Appleton), Dusty's Full Time Country Saloon (Menasha), ICU [Intensive Care Unit] Lounge (Neenah), Someplace (Eagle), Slip-Er-In (Delafield), The Recovery Room (La Crosse), Sit'N Bull (Cataract), Lizard Lounge (Oshkosh), Twisted Sisters (Sobieski), and Emotional Rescue (Beaver Dam). But the absolute winner has to be Louie's Godzilla Lounge and Ancient Chinese Tavern in Milwaukee.

▼ ▼ ▼ ▼ ▼ ▼ ▼ ▼ ▼ ▼ ▼ ▼ ▼ ▼ ▼ ▼ ▼ ▼

Shorewood
Village Pub
4488 N. Oakland Avenue
(414) 961-9879

This north shore spot has built up a solid reputation for quality scotch, bourbon, and cigars (if the names Arturo Fuente, Macanudo, and Don Tomas don't mean anything to you, well, it's not 50-cent stogie country). But many have overlooked the respectable beer collection of over 100 micros and imports. The micros do well by Wisconsin's fledgling breweries, and the imports represent a busman's holiday of Germany, the Netherlands, Belgium, and the British Isles.

Wall murals depicting Wisconsin history provide a backdrop for the sports crowd often gathered around five TV screens. The fans and patrons are well informed about sports and follow their teams closely. While the crowd is heavily Shorewood-based, customers from the west and north 'burbs also drop in. Many appreciate the Village Pub's policy of carryouts until midnight.

Our beer and hospitality survey crew found the place a real gem for its location. We started with an impression that everything in Shorewood had to be snooty and stuffy. Well, you don't have to go far to find places like that. The Village Pub may be the exception that proves the rule. Maybe not. In this refuge we met people who were modest and unassuming in spite of their resources and credentials. One of my bolder companions suggested that these customers were really just the domestics for the upscale crowd that lives in Shorewood.

That assertion was countered by a long and convoluted tale by a Village Pub patron who perversely defended his honor by claiming he had married into money. He went on to tell us a chilling story of loveless marriage to a heartless crone and the endless demands placed upon him. We almost asked him to run away with us. Turned out he was totally pulling our legs; his companions identified him as a dirt-poor Appalachian boy who made his own fortune and had a wife half his age. So methinks "gotcha" is a game known in this spot.

▼ ▼ ▼ ▼ ▼ ▼ ▼ ▼ ▼ ▼ ▼ ▼ ▼ ▼ ▼ ▼ ▼ ▼ ▼ ▼

Stonebank

Stone Bank Pub and Eatery
N67 W33395 Highway K
(262) 966-1975

Milwaukeeans sneak away to this hidden gem in the far reaches of Waukesha County and try to keep it a secret. The subterfuge has not worked well; those pesky brewing trade rags blew the cover. Still, it is a bit of a task to reach. Many reach it via Highway 16 west of Hartford and thence to Highway C north along Okauchee Lake until you reach Highway K. And a nice drive it is for the city-weary.

Its reputation is built on the 15 imports on tap, with good German representation. The moderate-size bottled collection also catches many recognizable imports and micros. Its repeat customers include quite a few folks who like to rotate their way through the selections (people after my own heart). Regulars believe that this pub is a good place for cocktails, too.

The social scene at the Stone Bank is dominated by the "Thursday Night Stomp," an eclectic mix of solo musicians and small bands. The big event of the year is the September Import and Micro Fest. If you're a micro fan, this is a prime place to meet old buddies and make new ones. The attendees are primarily Milwaukee metro, but the word is getting out in Madison and the Fox Valley. It's more intimate than the regional fests and makes a nice combo with a recreational overnight trip.

Speaking of which, the Stone Bank is strategically sited for those who wish to explore both the northern and southern units of Kettle Moraine. Thus the Stone Bank is beginning to see hikers, trail bikers, and nature gazers of various stripes. Find a good B&B in the area (I'll bet the tavern keepers can steer you to one) and you're set for day trips to Old World Wisconsin, Aztalan, Horicon, and the Hoard dairy museum. Or you can follow the antiques-and-collectibles circuit like some of the couples I encountered here.

One group relished their beers and their accounts of several days of flea markets, shops, and estate auctions. One beer evoked the tale of the group members unknowingly bidding against each other. The second beer spawned the narrative of misreading the antiques price guide and discovering that they had paid a price befitting the original instead of the replica now in their possession. But the third beer lubricated the mellow satisfaction of finding a long-lost treasure.

▾ ▾ ▾ ▾ ▾ ▾ ▾ ▾ ▾ ▾ ▾ ▾ ▾ ▾ ▾ ▾ ▾ ▾

Verona

Riley Tavern
8205 Riley Road
(just off Highway J and Military Ridge Trail)
(608) 845-9150

Don't let the address fool you. This is perhaps Dane County's most revered rural tavern, and it has not yet been overtaken by the sprawl and trophy houses that plague the area. The Riley Tavern long served neighboring farmers and the stray hunter or two. But the Military Ridge Trail brought new customers in bicyclist garb.

From the beer drinkers' perspective, the Riley Tavern is a welcome departure from the country bar surrender to Coors and Budweiser. Here we have a respectable sampler of southcentral Wisconsin beer: Berghoff, Esser, Garten Brau, and New Glarus. It also continues to curry favor with the old-timers by stocking Blatz and Old Milwaukee. Check out the changing bumper sticker collection on the beer cooler.

The bike trail crew also required that the Riley Tavern improve on typical tavern standards for nonalcoholic beverages. Biking families are an important part of that crowd, so there is a selection of mineral water, caffeine-free pop, and juice. A light menu of sandwiches and soup specials satisfies appetites. Surprises pop up on the Friday menu.

Fridays and Saturdays sometimes bring crowds taxing Riley Tavern's facilities. This is especially true on music nights. A blues band on a summer night can mean overflow crowds sitting on the grass outside listening to the music. But it is a congenial outdoor concert atmosphere in which leather-clad bikers and suburban moms get along fine.

I'm still partial to the Riley on its lazier and hazier afternoons. The place is quiet, held down by some grizzled locals who love to tease visiting bicyclists, and altogether fit for the contemplation of a tall, cool one. This is an indispensable stop on the local "tour de bars" that includes Pine Bluff, Blue Mounds, and Ridgeway. Many a line of biker (we're talking Hog version) bar lore has been slammed down by bards of the Harley-Davidson school.

▼ ▼ ▼ ▼ ▼ ▼ ▼ ▼ ▼ ▼ ▼ ▼ ▼ ▼ ▼ ▼ ▼ ▼ ▼

Whitewater

Randy's Fun Hunters Brewery

841 E. Milwaukee Street
(262) 473-8000

R andy's occupies a location that has served thirsty and hungry travelers since the end of Prohibition. Additions, remodeling, and changes in ownership almost every generation have not lessened its following among those taking the Highway 12 tour from northern Illinois to Madison. Although the bar was more or less adjunct to Randy's restaurant until a 1989 fire, the addition of brew pub facilities put the liquid refreshment end of the business on equal footing with the food and banquet side.

Recent housebrews include: amber lager, wheat ale, oatmeal stout, and pale ale. Call to check availability and for seasonal surprises. It seems like UW-Whitewater students and faculty always get the jump on me and drink up the new offerings before I get there.

There is a hearty little band of homebrewers who make this a home away from home. If you run into them you'll find some of them picky beyond all belief, but still finding brews among Randy's that get their seal of approval. Maybe it's kind of a game to them. Maybe they were pimping me by goading me into a defense of Berghoff, New Glarus, and Brewery Creek beers (all of which need no defense). If they mess with you, tell them to start their own damn brewpub.

As for food, customers give Randy's very high marks. The menu is extensive: 35 entrees, salads, sandwiches, a baked French onion soup specialty, and many appetizers. Daily specials, weekend prime rib, and Sunday brunch round out the well-received fare. This is one of those places where beer lovers start to worry that the food will take the spotlight away from the beer. Well, we won't let that happen, will we?

Southwest
Wisconsin

When southwest Wisconsin is mentioned, geologists and outdoors-people immediately think of the state's unglaciated driftless region and the coulees of the Mississippi River valley. According to the information put out for visitors by the Department of Tourism, this region of the state is a mix of driftless topography with some of Wisconsin's central sands and a bit of prairie country thrown in.

In many ways it is the area least familiar to travelers. Yet its boundaries include such well-known destinations as the House on the Rock and the Lake Delton attractions just west of Wisconsin Dells. It is a historic and long-settled area of Wisconsin, although it remains predominantly rural and can claim only La Crosse as a larger city.

Some tavern-savvy observers believe that it is the area least friendly to taverns, the recent past offering the anomaly of "dry" towns in Wisconsin and overzealous regulators of all stripes. But it is a rule happily eroded by the exceptions of lively tavern culture in places like Blanchardville, Highland, Hollandale, Muscoda, New Glarus, and Ridgeway, and the impressive party reputation of La Crosse.

The mixed reputation may have something to do with history and settlement patterns. It is the Wisconsin area least German and Nordic, with many of its earliest pioneers originating in the upper South. Yet its unusual ethnic stew of Scots, Welsh, and Cornish were known to hoist a brew or two after a day in the region's lead mines. So much so that the rough-and-tumble of those mining towns attracted many a reforming preacher. Strong antitavern sentiment in some churches continues to color local politics in parts of the region.

These historical factors notwithstanding, there are still plenty of taverns worthy of note, a great deal of beer-drinking tradition, and some positive trends. A lightly populated area that has lost many of its farms and cheese factories, it is fortunate to retain many of its classic rural taverns. It boasts a history of Wisconsin's first brewery (Mineral Point), the ruins of a once renowned regional brewery (Potosi), and the home of the state's longest-surviving brewery (Joseph Huber in Monroe).

In many parts of the area, the unfriendliness of conservative rural town government resulted in a clustering of taverns in the villages and small cities. This in turn added taverns to the list of "going into town" spots for rural dwellers and created routines of after-milking breakfast specials that persist in many taverns. The clustering has also created an informal pattern of pub crawling that is common on Friday, Saturday, and holiday nights. Called "cruising," "making the rounds," "doing the strip," and other names, the custom leads patrons to circulate between taverns that are within walking distance.

The clusters of village taverns also take on added life during the many festivals that southwest Wisconsin hosts. Check your visitor guides for calendars of events relating to mushroom gathering, apple harvest, antique farm equipment field days, and frontier reenactments. If you don't mind crowds, those are good days to check out taverns. The La Crosse Oktoberfest is in a class by itself and

▼ ▼ ▼ ▼ ▼ ▼ ▼ ▼ ▼ ▼ ▼ ▼ ▼ ▼ ▼ ▼ ▼ ▼

unrivaled in Wisconsin as a time when the spirit of the community event infuses both the festival grounds and the city's many taverns.

The river town taverns often augment the standard Wisconsin Friday night fish fry with catfish and snapping turtle. Some bars in the Mineral Point area offer the Cornish pasty. Taverns in the area are beginning to expand their offerings of beer and food to cater to visitors. Those in search of deer, turkey, trout, and antiques all have favorite spots. Canoeists, boaters, trail bicyclists, and campers are also a growing part of the customer base in prime recreation zones.

Southwest Wisconsin offers a number of motor routes for tavern touring. Highway 35 from Prairie du Chien to Fountain City is not only a scenic section of the Great River Road, it is also a belt of visitor-friendly taverns. Shorter routes, such as Sauk City–Spring Green–Muscoda and Mineral Point–Hollandale–New Glarus–Monroe, can also position you well for scenic touring and visits to friendly watering holes.

A note of caution: Southwest Wisconsin has more miles of curvy road and unguarded hillside dropoffs than the rest of the state combined. Deer, livestock, farm equipment, and bikers also make driving tricky. Be careful out there.

▼ ▼ ▼ ▼ ▼ ▼ ▼ ▼ ▼ ▼ ▼ ▼ ▼ ▼ ▼ ▼ ▼ ▼

Black River Falls

Molly's Grill

44 Main Street
(715) 284-9284

We tavern devotees are sometimes resistant to change in our favored habitats. This is probably even more true when we have a spot we visit infrequently. Such is the case with my interaction with Molly's in Black River Falls, a town that I must usually buzz by on the interstate. So when I make my semi-annual visit the changes that were made incrementally seem more abrupt.

Changes here probably bring the place more into line with expectations flowing from the name and the location. It definitely has settled into being a "grill," with less of a "bistro," "cafe," or "deli" feel than in the past. The plaster was taken down to expose brick and there's a fresh coat of paint. Co-owner Jeff explains that it was difficult to keep quality up on the massive number of entries, pastries, and dairy bar items. Gone too is the extensive Italian menu.

But what is left is still impressive by tavern standards: ten sandwich plates, six burgers, a diverse salad selection, six dinners, plenty of appetizers, and nightly specials. Not to mention a great fish fry, Pioneer Beer Bread, and Pioneer brews on tap.

The bar side of the business remains solid and well managed. There is still good conversation to be had under the watchful eyes of a Sampson poolhall painting. It's still a place to meet colorful characters and hear yarns about the area. On my last visit it was an earthy Ho Chunk mother-daughter duo fresh off a shift at the casino who kept me in stitches for hours.

Molly's has quietly built a reputation among outdoorspeople who spent their free time on the waters and in the woods of Jackson County. It's a heck of a treat after roughing it.

▼ ▼ ▼ ▼ ▼ ▼ ▼ ▼ ▼ ▼ ▼ ▼ ▼ ▼ ▼ ▼ ▼ ▼

Boscobel Hotel
1005 Wisconsin Avenue
(608) 375-4714

While travelers may have known this historic site in its former lives, they may not be aware that new owners Jeff and Beth Novinska have undertaken an impressive remodeling job. Some may lament the passing of the blues jams and the solo acoustic guitar acts, but the regulars still keep the spot as congenial a one as you'll find between Muscoda and Prairie du Chien.

As for history, the substantial stone building is a fine example of the first wave of hotels that replaced the ramshackle inns and boardinghouses of early statehood days. The building also has a place in legend and lore. On the prim and proper side, it boasts its status as the birthplace of the Gideon Bible. On the more titillating side, the locals insist that John and Jackie Kennedy conceived a child in an upstairs room during a campaign swing.

The Boscobel Hotel's bar sticks to bottled beer, with roughly 20 types available at any given time. Southern Wisconsin's regionals and micros are usually in the mix. The Novinskas have also reintroduced food for the first time since the hotel's heyday as a lodging place. At my last 1999 visit the menu was still in the experimental and expanding stage but did include locally praised sandwiches and steaks.

Nearly everyone in the lower Wisconsin River valley has a Boscobel Hotel story. Back-to-the-landers from rural Blue River like to recall times in the mid-1980s when two Sandinistas from Nicaragua would visit with a group of weekly newspaper writers, American Indians, and antiforeclosure farm activists. Long-time residents cherish heirloom stories of soldiers seeing off or welcoming back five generations of soldiers. The place is so steeped in history that during the annual Boscobel festival, Civil War reenactors seem like part of the furnishings.

▼ ▼ ▼ ▼ ▼ ▼ ▼ ▼ ▼ ▼ ▼ ▼ ▼ ▼ ▼ ▼ ▼ ▼

Dodgeville

Dino's
110 Diagonal Street
(608) 935-9380

The bar-trained eye will detect that this site was formerly Pat & Mike's. Physically the place remains the same, except that the pool table is gone in order to accommodate more tables for diners. But there is a shift in emphasis and constituency here as well.

Some of the beer selection has been trimmed, especially the bottled line. Anchoring the taps are Guinness and several New Glarus selections. Guest appearances by Leinie's and other regionals also pop up on occasion. Pat James, a stalwart in the Great Tavern Tour, tends bar here three nights a week.

The food, already solid under Pat & Mike's regime, has broadened in hours and selections. They make their own pizzas now and deliver locally. Co-owners Linda and Dean divide the duties, with Linda in the primary hands-on role. Catch her when things aren't so busy and you'll find she's got a whole skeleton of funny bones.

Finding a not-busy time isn't easy. That is one major change that came with the change in ownership. The pace is a bit more hectic, the crowd more youthful, and the noise level significantly higher. The happy hour is often wall-to-wall with patrons. So those touchy about such things should plan on an early lunch visit or mid-afternoon stop.

While in the area you'll want to visit the Pleasant Ridge Store (actually a country tavern) five miles north of Dodgeville on Highway Z and Riha's and Murphy's Log Cabin in Hollandale. Be careful on Highway 191, they say it's haunted.

▼ ▼ ▼ ▼ ▼ ▼ ▼ ▼ ▼ ▼ ▼ ▼ ▼ ▼ ▼ ▼ ▼ ▼

Ferryville

Sportsman's Bar and Grill
Highway 35
(608) 734-3563

There must be hundreds of Wisconsin taverns bearing this name (I've been in several dozen). Many are exclusively male domains. This one will do quite nicely for a family visit, thank you. They keep things simple here with one tap beer (Pabst Blue Ribbon) and a handful of standard brands. And they sell almost as much pop as beer.

It has a fantastic view of the Mississippi River. Autumn leaves and migratory bird pilgrimages provide pleasant clashes of colors and motion. Rail buffs will enjoy the frequent Burlington Northern–Santa Fe action on the main line between the bar and the river. In season, hunters, fishermen, campers, and birdwatchers all pass through on what is called the longest one-street town in America.

Sportsman's is one of the better information spots on this stretch of the great river. Outside of Northwoods lake lodges, this is home to some of the most savvy fishermen in Wisconsin. But if there are six or more locals at the bar you can find out about more than fishing hot spots. Overheard on my last visit: who has apple butter to sell, where to find smoked fish, how to find quilters and potters hidden in the hills, where turkeys are foraging on the bluffs, and which civic group is sponsoring a turtle dinner.

This establishment ranks high on my tall tale index, and I don't just mean fishing stories. Tavern tales thrown my way in this space have included ghosts, legendary trappers, madams of yesteryear, and UFOs. But it absolutely stands out in a category of its own for a chilling tale of a family of local witches.

A café-style menu starts pulling in customers at 6 A.M. The hearty breakfasts are geared to the hunting and fishing crowd. The boating crowd stops in for drinks and sandwiches at lunch. Tourists on the Great River Road (Highway 35) round out the day at dinnertime. The food is standard fare but prepared and served in surroundings cleaner than most "sportsmen's" bars. The catfish dinner has a reputation that reaches from Prairie du Chien to La Crosse.

Fountain City

Monarch Tavern and Preservation Hall

19 N. Main Street

(608) 687-4231

The origins of the Monarch as an Odd Fellows all-male club accounts for the "No Waitresses Since 1894—Order at the Bar" sign. But rest assured, hospitality and gender inclusiveness have improved since then. The 10 P.M. unannounced arrival of our tavern touring group (on its second wind after a visit to La Crosse's Oktoberfest) was met not with a groan but with the re-opening of the kitchen.

We ate at refinished saloon poker tables, quaffed the beers available at that time, and listened to the folk music wafting out of the Preservation Hall dining area. We sampled the contract-brewed Fountain Brew and Prairie Moon Red and pronounced them top-shelf. Since that visit Old Heidelberg, Eagle Valley Harvest Gold, and Fountain Bock have come online. The glowing reports continue.

The place is also gaining fame as an all-around community center, entertainment spot, and visitors' information bureau. The arts run to some alternative fare, with folk music and jazz making a rare small-town appearance. A mention of the spot sent a bike-touring friend on her own expedition. She was pleased to add her endorsement along with a report of memorable conversations with local artists, potters, photographers, and musicians.

The Monarch fits perfectly in this picturesque Mississippi River town. The owners proudly distribute the local boosters walking tour flyer. In good weather, they also cheerfully usher patrons to the beer garden with the river valley view, in spite of the long walk for servers. In a place that has everything to commend it, special note must be made of Bert the cook. It just doesn't get much better than Prairie Moon Red and Bert's Famous Ribs. So come on, Wisconsinites, discover what the good folks from Rochester, Minnesota, have already been sampling on our soil.

La Crosse

Bodega Brew Pub
122 South Fourth Street
(608) 782-0677

Bodega possesses the distinct advantage of a location in the heart of one of the best tavern districts in Wisconsin. The day time business and student crowd gives way to evening beer drinkers and seekers of jazz and progressive contemporary music. Two full-windowed walls make it the best spot for people watching in Wisconsin's favorite party town. It is ranked above Madison's State Street as the place for post-collegiate types to perform spectator sipping.

In the first edition of this guide it was mentioned that the in-house brewing apparatus was undergoing extensive modification. Happily, the clanging, banging, and adjustment is completed and beer pours forth. Local hopheads have much to be pleased about with the "Downtown Brown." The porter, rolled oat stout, and pale ale also hold their own.

In the meantime, there are still many treats to sample. The 11 taps with rotated selections do well by the brews pouring forth from New Glarus and Berghoff, with due deference to local Old Style products. The bottled line is creeping up on 200 entries. Those offerings span the distance from Abbaye des Rois to Zywiec Pilsner. Even veteran brown bottle fans will run into new finds here among both imports and micros. Beer confidence runs so high at Bodega that they have no menu. A few of the bartenders have looked the other way at my smuggled sandwiches or burritos (my cover story is that I'm on a tight business trip schedule and have time for a tavern visit or diner stop, not both).

The Bodega is well situated for LaCrosse pub crawls. Aside from being in the heart of the tavern action the location is accessible to lodgings, restaurants, and entertainment. It's not a stretch to say that you're within walking distance of two dozen bars. Some say LaCrosse is one of the best places for a weekend getaway for couples. There's the clean and safe downtown, the shops, and, in warm weather, the riverfront festivals and riverboat rides. Throw in Octoberfest and you have a well-deserved reputation for good times.

La Crosse

Night Hawks Tap Room
401 S. Third Street
(608) 785-7427

Seven taps with rotating selections pull in the beer drinkers. Wheat beers were hot on my last summer stop at this popular nightspot. And, oddly enough, here in Heileman town, bottled and draft Point beers have a following among the regulars. It has a growing selection of regional brews.

Night Hawks is the type of place that picks up more energy the later it gets. The crowd often grows after midnight. The live music mix includes blues, rock, funk, and more blues. A Wednesday blues jam provides local and national surprises. The band posters bedeck the walls like campaign ribbons.

Those who favor elbow-bending over toe-tapping needn't worry about being blasted out the door on band nights. Night Hawks has one of the best midsize club setups in terms of coexistence of the bar crowd and the music crowd. The bar area is separated from the rear room by a low arched passageway that acts as an acoustic block. If you venture through that portal on a busy night you'll want your dancing shoes.

There is a bit of an age and cultural divide between the front bar and the back dance floor. The bar patrons look to be in their 30s and 40s. The dancers are a bit younger. At the bar a jukebox collection of blues, salsa, jazz, zydeco, and fusion suggests a mellow broad-mindedness.

A bit of candor compels the admission that more than one observer among my mostly male corps of tavern sleuths has remarked that the bartenders here include, year in and year out, some of the most attractive young women in La Crosse. This demonstrates that some tavern owners will make extra efforts to differentiate themselves from the competition. It works here because the bartenders, both men and women, generally know what they're doing.

How about that lava lamp collection behind the bar?

ANOTHER ROUND

Boyer's Favorite Wisconsin Beers

1. Sprecher Amber
2. New Glarus Snowshoe Ale
3. Berghoff Lager
4. Sprecher Winter Brew
5. Green Bay Pub Draught Cream Ale
6. Leinenkugel Red
7. Point Maple Wheat
8. Berghoff Winterfest Hazelnut
9. Garten Brau Dark
10. Gray's Oatmeal Stout

▼ ▼ ▼ ▼ ▼ ▼ ▼ ▼ ▼ ▼ ▼ ▼ ▼ ▼ ▼ ▼ ▼ ▼

Mineral Point

Brewery Creek Inn and Pub

23 Commerce Street
(608) 987-3298
www.brewerycreek.com

B eer drinking in Wisconsin does not get any more history-steeped than
Brewery Creek. Just a mug's throw from the site of the first commercial
brewery in Wisconsin (circa 1830s). Up the street from the oldest railroad
depot in the state. Next door to the unique Foundry Bookstore, an emporium
of rare volumes, manuscripts, and maps of the age of exploration in the Old
Northwest Territory. Across the creek from the old haunted Walker House, site
of a territorial era hanging. Throw in a quaint town of antique and artisan shops
and historic Pendarvis and you'll have as fine a day trip as exists in these parts.

Brewery Creek's "inn" part of the business is a sumptuous bed and breakfast. Open since July 1997, the seven rooms with fireplaces, whirlpool baths,
and computer modems are heavily booked. Locally supplied farm produce and
a wood-fired bake oven make for interesting provisions. Visitors have raved
about the portobello mushroom sandwich, the cashew chicken sandwich, and
the daily special soups, and key lime pie.

Then there's beer. Mahogany ale, an amber, and a pleasing kolsch made up
the initial brews. Then along came porter, stout, alt, and sodas. In my humble
opinion the porter is one of the best I've had. They like to experiment here, so
call ahead to see what's on the drawing board. It should also be noted that
Brewery Creek is supplying beer to Billy's Roaring Twenties, a fine steakhouse
on U.S. Highway 151, east of Mineral Point.

While you're in Mineral Point make the High Street pub crawl. It's an interesting mix of shot and beer joints and restored 19th century buildings. I'm partial to Riki's and the Midway. Those who want to dip into the lead mining past
should drive five miles north on Highway 39 for a visit to the Pard Town Pub
in Linden.

The effort to run a quiet B & B makes for some limited hours in the brewpub. It is not unusual to find them closed at 10 PM even on Saturday night.
Make this stop part of a day trip plan or call ahead for evening hours. The oper-
ators here, the Donughue family, have really gotten the hang of this operation.
Jeff is really starting to look comfortable behind that bar.

▼ ▼ ▼ ▼ ▼ ▼ ▼ ▼ ▼ ▼ ▼ ▼ ▼ ▼ ▼ ▼ ▼

Monroe

Baumgartner's Cheese Store and Tavern
1023 16th Avenue
(608) 325-6157

It doesn't get any more Wisconsin than cheese and beer. Throw in a little leberwurst and, some would say, you have the quintessential tavern of the Badger state. Oddly enough, many in nearby Illinois would agree. Thus the anomaly that one of Wisconsin's best known and most beloved taverns is not familiar to Wisconsin tavern fans outside the south-central part of the state.

Baumgartner's is, in a way, the homebase for the Huber/Berghoff lines. They probably tap out more Huber and Huber Bock than any other bar in the world. Berghoff is well represented with 3 to 5 taps depending on the season, including brews that are not seen on tap elsewhere. Bottled New Glarus and Grays brews are also on hand.

The sociology of Baumgartner's is as impressive as the tavern's credentials. On weekdays there is a sizable lunch crowd. The nights belong to serious beer drinkers. I have seen nine pitchers of beer on the bar for ten patrons on a Friday night. But never fear, the crowd is well mannered. On Saturday, the tourists — from motorhome tourers to Golden Wing motorcyclists — take over. One still hears an occasional comment dropped in schweitzer deitsch (Swiss German dialect), though not like years ago. "Buebe" marks the men's room just as it does in many Schtubbe in the Alps. Swiss maps, heralds, and murals decorate the walls.

And the cheese! The front of the building handles the retail and mail order trade. The tavern specialty is the sturdy cheese sandwich: brick, cheddar, Swiss and the not for the timid limburger. Combination sandwiches feature hard salami or braunschweiger. Even the deli-style sandwiches come with a slice of brick on the side. The store portion also offers gruyere, baby Swiss, gouda, edam, havarti, and an award-winning pesto cheese with basil and pine nuts.

The real test of intestinal fortitude comes in the form of the ultimate Monroe sandwich: limburger, braunschweiger, raw onion, and horseradish mustard on rye. Darn tasty with a pint of Berghoff Maibock. And, oddly enough, the subject of some ribald remarks that do not bear repeating in a guidebook.

Owner John Huber (yes, those Hubers of brewing fame) presides over the fun with warmth and hospitality. Hit the place on the right Saturday night and he'll introduce you to the homebrewers who meet in his place and will brief you on Monroe's tavern scene.

Monroe

Veterans of Foreign Wars— Post 2312

1428 17th Street
(608) 325-3338

C heck out this place while the "greatest generation" is still around to tell you about the seminal events of the Twentieth Century. That goes double for you whippersnappers who didn't have childhoods shaped by parents and uncles just a few years back from convoys, beach landings, and bomb runs. It was in such places as Post 2312 that those men, and some women, came for decades to renew those bonds forged in a crucible of depression and global war.

The Post's bar is open to the public and serves up one of Monroe's favorite fish fries. Though most of the vets drink the standard brands, the Post bar is a hometown loyal with a rotating Berghoff tap. The operation is ably administered by a former Chicago and Northwestern brakeman, Post quartermaster Bob Pickett. Debbie, the live wire weekend bartender, keeps the customers on their toes.

The Post bar is located along what use to be known as Smokey Row. This is the bar strip outside of the downtown. In its prime the street bustled with railroaders, shippers, and the comings and goings of travelers. The neighborhood is no longer smoky from the old steam locomotives and the whistle is heard no more. But it is clearly a neighborhood with lots of memories.

The same rules that I outline for Legion Post 100 in Sparta apply here in Monroe. It is generally not a good idea to pontificate aggressively about things that one does not know from direct experience in such places. You'll find World War II vets to be a more diverse lot than those who have since served in uniform. But they don't tolerate a lot of moral relativity, they saw evil and whipped its butt. Buy them a drink!

▼ ▼ ▼ ▼ ▼ ▼ ▼ ▼ ▼ ▼ ▼ ▼ ▼ ▼ ▼ ▼ ▼

Muscoda

Nordic Inn
Junction of Highways 60 and 80
(on the north bank of the Wisconsin River)
(608) 739-3150

Want to rub elbows and bend elbows with loggers? Southwest Wisconsin's hardwood loggers have a reputation for knowing the best taverns in the area. A logging rig in a bar's parking lot, like a semi in front of a café, is supposed to be a good omen. Tavern patrons in the Muscoda area find even more comfort in the fact that the Kever logging family took over the Nordic Inn. Sam and Lynette Kever have brought stability and new features to the Nordic Inn after a number of ownership changes.

A onetime favorite among outdoor enthusiasts, the Nordic Inn's offerings of food, lodging, and drink failed to fire on all cylinders in the mid-1990s. After the Kevers' takeover in 1997, hunters, fishermen, canoeists, and snowmobilers found the earlier full range of service restored and improved upon. Motel bars are seldom worthy of note and rarely rate praise beyond sparing weary travelers the hassles of going out in the evening. But the Kevers have created a genuine tavern environment that draws local patrons from a four-county area.

The beer selection varies and is based primarily on the national brands. However, there are usually a number of Wisconsin regional beers and at least one good draft beer available. Draft root beer is also sold by the mug. The restaurant started out serving only the breakfast and lunch trade, but popular demand soon had it offering the traditional Friday and Saturday night one-two punch of fish and prime rib. The locals love it. Show up at the right time in May and you may see morel mushrooms on the menu.

The location is great—only a hundred yards from the north bank of the Wisconsin River (across from the Village of Muscoda). It is the closest tavern to the river west of Sauk City. It sits at the junction of two of southern Wisconsin's great touring roads: Highway 60 from Prairie du Sac to Prairie du Chien and Highway 80 from Hillsboro to Hazel Green.

Necedah

Star Route Lounge
Highway 21 West
(608) 565-2461

Patrons of the Star Route Lounge know the marsh country. The place draws a robust crowd formed by the tough economic realities of the central sands region. Outdoorspeople of all stripes stop in, but the bow hunter contingent seems particularly strong. Thus, Star Route is not the place for you if you are offended by the sight of bloodied hunting knives strapped to camouflage-clad legs. In season, there are few places where the hunting stories run as thick and as colorful.

Locals head here for steaks and Leinie's Red. The second meal of choice after a day in the woods is the "Gator Kabob," a combination of vegetables, beef, pork, and alligator. Regulars also praise the fresh-cut french fries.

It appears that there is generally a differentiation in the crowd at Star Route: nondrinkers do not sit at the bar and nurse sodas or coffee. These milder pursuits are relegated to the dining area. The beer and brandy drinkers hold sway at the bar and are often exuberant. Those with delicate ears should be forewarned about occasional rough language, but it doesn't appear personalized or threatening.

There is no desire to be trendy here. Strangers still buy each other drinks here. The bartender will sell you a camouflage shirt if you need one. And if you are in the mood, you can drop quarters in the jukebox and play some polkas.

The culture is more central sands than driftless, with the feel of swamps, tamaracks, and jack pines oozing out of the hardscrabble bachelors who make their weekly tavern pilgrimage here and to other scattered backcountry bars in Juneau County. They love to regale visitors with stories about city folk swallowed up by the marshes. They even steered me to a cute story about a half man, half pig creature said to inhabit the abandoned farms near Sprague.

▼ ▼ ▼ ▼ ▼ ▼ ▼ ▼ ▼ ▼ ▼ ▼ ▼ ▼ ▼ ▼ ▼ ▼

New Diggings General Store and Inn
2944 County Hignway I (at Highway W)
(608) 965-3231

Southwest Wisconsin has a venerable tradition of store tavern spots that combined both functions from the outset or that evolved from stores into taverns. Here in a forgotten corner of Wisconsin, there is a clear feeling that such establishments are the descendants of the early territorial trading posts. The New Diggings General Store and Inn is only a few miles from where Jesse Shull set up the Old Ouiskonsin Fort and Trading Post for the Hudson Bay Company in the early 1820s.

The antique and collectible furnishings lend to the feeling of historical continuity. The large cast-iron woodstove in the middle of the main bar space warms patrons in the cold parts of the year, while the warm season finds them outside in a beer garden surrounded by the abandoned ghost town buildings of New Diggings.

This beer-only tavern is almost better known by Dubuque, Iowa, and Galena, Illinois, residents than by Wisconsinites. They come for the music and easy sociability. Bands play every Saturday night (9 P.M. to 1 A.M.) and Sunday afternoon (3:30 P.M. to 7:30 P.M.). No tap beer, but a bottled lineup that includes the standard big brands plus Leinie's, Berghoff, New Glarus, Sam Adams, Harp, and jugs of Mississippi Mud Black and Tan.

They're very history-minded at the General Store and Inn, offering books for sale on local traditions and dispensing legend and lore. Their motto is "where the moon is always full," suggesting both the celebratory mood of the establishment and the mythic quality of a town that in the 1830s had a bigger population than Chicago in those days. Now, New Diggings is down to a few houses, a group of dilapidated buildings, and two taverns. That's right, across from the General Store and Inn is another "General Store" that serves a somewhat younger crowd and confuses first-time visitors. That's OK—it's worth a visit, too.

▼ ▼ ▼ ▼ ▼ ▼ ▼ ▼ ▼ ▼ ▼ ▼ ▼ ▼ ▼ ▼ ▼ ▼ ▼

New Glarus
Puempel's Olde Tavern
18 6th Avenue
(608) 527-2045
www.puempels.com

In this little Swiss burg it is no small matter to pick amongst taverns. So, darn it, you'll just have to try them all. But my advice is to start at Puempel's, that's what my friends from Germany do when they're in Green County. And that's a rare consensus among Christian Democrats, Social Democrats, and Greens.

This is really what Wisconsin taverns are all about: a long bar, stools in military formation, and congenial service. Owners Chuck and Lisa Bigler have it running like the proverbial Swiss watch.

The offerings are simple, yet solid. They are known for soups and sandwiches. Being Green County you can count on cheese and sausage. Beerwise, there are only three taps, but two are devoted to hometown New Glarus brews (there's also Coors light for the heathens). In addition, the entire bottled lines of New Glarus and Huber/Berghoff are usually available.

They have a great after work crowd of locals. My tavern buddies say that the best time to come is in the off-season when the tourists are safely back in the flatlands. That's prime time for a New Glarus pub crawl and lodgings are more readily available. You'll want to make the rounds of the Sportsman's Bar & Grill, Burreson's, and Jimmy's (home of local blues jam and the Edel Pils Orchestra).

While New Glarus ties in well with a Monroe trip, the old Swiss settlement merits a visit overnight on its own. They've got good restaurants, bakeries, museums, and a brewery to visit. The town also hosts the Vietnam Veteran Winterfest R & R in late January, with a great bonfire.

▼ ▼ ▼ ▼ ▼ ▼ ▼ ▼ ▼ ▼ ▼ ▼ ▼ ▼ ▼ ▼ ▼ ▼ ▼

Platteville

Hoist House
90 N. Second Street
(608) 348-7819

Downtown Platteville has as hefty a district of college bars as any of the smaller cities hosting University of Wisconsin system campuses. UW-Platteville students are a major influence in many of these spots, but not so much that older nonacademic types are unwelcome. That's especially true of the Hoist House, which draws beer drinkers from surrounding towns like Lancaster, Fennimore, and Mineral Point.

Over the last several years, they've steadily added taps until they're now at 11. The usual lineup includes Grays, multiple Leinie's, Berghoff, Sam Adams, Woodchuck Draft Cider, and macrobrews. The coolers hold approximately 30 imports.

The "hoist" in the establishment's name is a reference to the crude elevators in the area's old lead and zinc mines. The vintage tile floor and stamped metal ceiling lends credence to the many stories of the Hoist House serving as a rough and tumble pre-Prohibition bar which could be exited via a tunnel. A few of the regulars mentioned that prior generations of UW-Platteville alumni would remember the tavern as a party bar called the Black Cat.

The routine for a Platteville pub crawl with the Hoist House as a starting point varies depending on your age and academic standing. Hoist House is one of the few spots that draws both a wide age spectrum and a fair town and gown sampling. The over thirty crowd often gravitates to the veterans posts and supper clubs. Those comfortable in the student mix usually stay right in the tavern district clustered in the few blocks around the Hoist House.

There is history aplenty in this small city, with an interesting museum and regional collections at the library of UW-Platteville. Nearby you have the First Capitol site near Belmont and it's just a hop, skip, and a jump over to Potosi with its venerated brewery site.

▼ ▼ ▼ ▼ ▼ ▼ ▼ ▼ ▼ ▼ ▼ ▼ ▼ ▼ ▼ ▼ ▼ ▼ ▼ ▼

ANOTHER ROUND
Beer Events in Wisconsin

Be sure to call ahead for the exact dates.

January
Ice Cold Brewers Fest
Minocqua (715) 358-3040

February
Beer Lovers Brewfest
Manitowoc (920) 683-3926

March
Blessing of the Bock
Milwaukee (414) 645-1580

April
Gitchee Gumee Beer Fest
Superior (715) 394-7716

May
Point's Spring Festival of Beers
Stevens Point (715) 344-9310

Northeast Wisconsin Beer Festival
Appleton (920) 731-3322

Wisconsin Microbrewers Fest
Chilton (920) 849-2534

June
Summerfest (last week of June
and first week of July)
Milwaukee (414) 273-FEST

Southport Micro Beer Festival
Kenosha (262) 694-9050

Essen Haus Bierfest
Madison (608) 258-8619

July
Jaycees Brews and Blues Festival
Oshkosh (920) 235-0605

Wisconsin State Fair
West Allis (800) 884-FAIR

Germanfest
Milwaukee (414) 464-9444

August
Great Taste of the Midwest
Madison (608) 249-7126

West Bend Germanfest
West Bend (262) 338-2666

September
Sprecherfest
Milwaukee (414) 297-8000

Taste of Madison
Madison (608) 831-1725

Green Bay Oktoberfest (late September)
Green Bay (920) 437-BEER

Boulder Beer Fest
Boulder Junction (715) 356-9456

Harvest Fair
Milwaukee (414) 266-7000

Appleton Octoberfest
Appleton (920) 734-3377

Gemuetlichkeit Homebrew Competition
Jefferson (920) 674-3843

October
La Crosse Oktoberfest
(sometimes starts late September)
La Crosse (608) 784-FEST

Quivey's Grove Beer Fest
Madison (608) 273-4900

Rhinelander Oktoberfest
Rhinelander (800) 236-4386

New Glarus Oktoberfest
New Glarus (800) 527-6838

November
Taste of the World
Green Bay (920) 437-0202

▼ ▼ ▼ ▼ ▼ ▼ ▼ ▼ ▼ ▼ ▼ ▼ ▼ ▼ ▼ ▼ ▼

Pleasant Ridge

Pleasant Ridge Store
4948 Highway Z (5 mioes north of Dodgeville at intersection of Z and ZZ)
(608) 935-1013

This tucked away spot has become one of the favorite rural haunts of tavern tourers. Proprietors Sue and Charlie took a venerable general store and turned it into a great spot for year-round visiting. Along the way they built up a loyal following of local farmers, campers at Governor Dodge State Park, fishermen, and deer and turkey hunters.

Nearly every month brings new developments to this rustic tavern on the back roads between Spring Green and Dodgeville. The building has expanded, a deck was added, an outdoor grove reclaimed, and a brand spanking new kitchen added to broaden the menu. Throw in music jams of bluegrass, folk, and blues, along with an outdoor summer music fest, and you have all the fixings for a good time.

Like so many forgotten crossroads in southwest Wisconsin, Pleasant Ridge is a remnant of a pioneer settlement. While only the tavern and a converted schoolhouse offer testimony to this past, good stories are still congenially told about days gone by. Supposedly the ghost of the Pleasant Ridge Peddler, a murder victim of the wild mining days, still wanders the nearby ridge and valleys and, sometimes, causes a spring to run red.

At this time Sue and Charlie are serving only bottled beer, but what a nice selection for a rural spot. They dispense plenty of New Glarus, Berghoff and Capitol here, not to mention Leinie's, Guinness, Pacifico, and all the megabrews. What's more the barrel of roasted peanuts in the shell hardly ever runs out. Planned additions of beer taps and an esteemed chef in the kitchen will make the place darn near country perfect.

▼ ▼ ▼ ▼ ▼ ▼ ▼ ▼ ▼ ▼ ▼ ▼ ▼ ▼ ▼ ▼ ▼ ▼

Prairie du Chien

Winneshiek Bar and Marina

Frenchtown Road

(608) 326-2888

Summer boating season enlivens many taverns along the Mississippi River. When the bar business goes hand in hand with a marina, the pace is even more frenetic. Boaters, construction workers, salespeople, and campers converge on the Winneshiek in conjunction with their daily rounds.

The bar and marina are of comparatively recent origin, the north fringe of Prairie du Chien being the focus of residential and commercial redevelopment. You might be surprised that the marina is not directly on the big river; Winneshiek is reached via a dredged channel and inlet. The site combines both the good and the bad of locations with growing pains: a nice view of the bluffs in Iowa contrasting with the somewhat neglected restaurant/campground business across the road and an out-of-place mobile home park sitting exposed on the north bank of the marina.

But this is not, after all, a resort. It's a refueling spot. Camping families stop in to get a break from cooking and to let kids watch the boats. Construction workers grab quick lunches. Boaters snatch up takeout food and beverages. Room enough inside and tables enough on an outside deck to serve them all, with space left over for a game to be played on a cribbage board built into the bar surface.

The fare is simple and the beer selection limited (with promises of expansion). The most popular brand of beer here is Ice Cold. Sandwiches for lunch, daily dinner specials, and Friday night fish fries meet boater expectations. The Philly Cheesesteak does not match what this native Pennsylvanian experienced at the hands of Mama Tallarico, but it clearly surpasses other tavern versions.

Note to parents: Winneshiek's is a family-friendly spot. But I did notice, on two separate occasions, that a large ship's figurehead of a bare-chested mermaid seems to startle small children.

▼ ▼ ▼ ▼ ▼ ▼ ▼ ▼ ▼ ▼ ▼ ▼ ▼ ▼ ▼ ▼ ▼

Prairie du Chien
The Main Entrance
2115 W. Blackhawk Avenue
(608) 326-4030
www.mainentrance.tripod.com

Prairie du Chien has just about the longest tavern tradition to be found in Wisconsin. First a French fur trading site, then a British military outpost, and finally home to the U.S. Army's Fort Crawford in territorial days, the settlement has been a site of rowdiness for over 300 years.

The Main Entrance carries on the long tradition of homespun fun in a thoroughly off-beat fashion. In sort of an inside joke, the sign always says "Live Music Tonight." Often that is not the case, but, in addition to booked weekend acts, there's a tradition of folks just showing up and playing in this funky location.

Mike Anderson presides over this friendly chaos with a mellow disposition and open door policy. As a result one can expect to find just about every breed of counterculture and alternative thinker in this joint. The place can seem like a real time machine at times and the time is about 1973, the year the place opened for business in its current form.

On the beverage front, the Main Entrance offers many surprises. They only run one tap, but it's usually something other than the national brands. The coolers offer selections as diverse as the customers: Hacker Pschorr, Spotted Cow, Capital varieties, the Leinie's line, Red Stripe, and Harp. Upon request, Mike even produced Rhinelander and Rhinelander Bock from the hidden cool recesses.

On the music front, there are unpredictable jams and occasional touring artists. So check the website. Locals are appreciative of local talent and come out to hear Eugene Shedivy's *Gene and the Woodticks*. Another Prairie favorite is founder and former owner John Burlingame whose poetic style does justice to his Bob Dylan and Phil Ochs renditions.

There's a decent little tavern tour to be made right in Prairie's downtown, especially if you're partial to simple neighborhood bars. It's a nice area to visit in summer and fall. The peak times are the Father's Day weekend frontier rendezvous and the New Year's Eve "Carp Drop," when a large frozen fish serves as the equivalent of the Times Square countdown ball.

▼ ▼ ▼ ▼ ▼ ▼ ▼ ▼ ▼ ▼ ▼ ▼ ▼ ▼ ▼ ▼ ▼ ▼

Reedsburg

Corner Pub
100 E. Main Street
(608) 524-8989

Travelers to Reedsburg have been bemoaning the closure of the Endehouse, the cutest little brewpub this side of Chilton. Well declare the mourning officially over, good beer is again flowing in central Sauk County. Surprise, surprise, one of the Petersons is involved with this fine enterprise.

Pete Peterson is at the helm and has plans to create a different ambience at his new joint. With the Corner Pub there will be sure and steady introduction to good beer. While some of the plans are still on the drawing board, there is intent to offer around 50 beers with a respectable number of bottled imports. It is also expected the summer 2002 will also be the shakedown of the in-house brewing setup.

Tavern fans are hopeful that Pete will educate area beer palates in this new setting. Initial regulars tend to be a bit younger and more blue collar than before, but the standards remain high.

If there is anything missing that some fans of Endehouse will notice it's the pare-down of food selections, with the menu staying on the burger and sandwich side of the tracks. But this guide is complied with the assumption that its readers will come down on the side of beer nine times out of ten.

]Make sure to include this spot on your lower Wisconsin River or Wisconsin Dells rambles. It's only twenty minutes from Spring Green via Highway 23. It's also a good jumping-off spot for explorations of rural taverns in places like Plain, Loganville, and Bear Valley.

▼ ▼ ▼ ▼ ▼ ▼ ▼ ▼ ▼ ▼ ▼ ▼ ▼ ▼ ▼ ▼ ▼ ▼

Legion Post 100 Bar
Highway 21 East
(608) 269-4411

In the Fort McCoy/Camp Douglas area there is no shortage of bars with retired military hardware permanently parked outside. The Army presence and
patriotic heartland values combine to make local veterans clubs a focus for
social life. It is an area where you might sit down to a fish fry in a room full of
camouflage fatigues. The person next to you is as likely to be a National Guard
officer, a reservist pilot, or a crusty career sergeant as a graying veteran of
Omaha Beach.

Sparta's Legion Post 100 Bar is the most representative area tavern catering
to GIs and veterans. Other local taverns may sport names like "The Foxhole" or
decorate with a military theme using combat photographs or ship and aircraft
posters, but Post 100 is open and accessible to nonveterans and nonmilitary
personnel. It is a site of receptions and homespun entertainment. They're also
generous enough to steer you to veterans clubs in Tomah or New Lisbon if a big
dance or benefit dinner will boost comrades in those towns.

Leinenkugel craft brews are the only beers to augment the national brands
and Heileman's lines in Post 100's coolers. But if you stop here it's as much for
the sociology as for the liquid refreshment. It is no secret that the veterans population is an aging one. At one time, many more American Legion and Veterans
of Foreign Wars posts had bars that were open to the public.

Twenty to 30 years ago, many of these veterans posts had bar regulars who
were none too friendly to strangers. Never mind that the only shooting these
bellicose types had witnessed was at the Fort Dix, New Jersey, rifle range. Long
hair, tie-dyed shirts, and alternative political views were not welcome, even if
the bearers of same were still nursing combat wounds. Thankfully, the internal
culture has changed for the better in most of these places (the ones that didn't
change closed for lack of business).

The Sparta post is perhaps unusual in that it hosts quite a few guardsmen,
reservists, and active-duty military in addition to veterans of prior wars, and is
still fairly accepting of the general public. This is not to say that the visitor won't
find some zealous views on foreign policy matters here. And some sensitivity is
called for if a talkative patron evokes a painful memory. A general rule of
thumb in such quarters goes thusly: if you do not know the event under discussion through firsthand experience, don't open your mouth about it.

Check out the military unit ceiling tiles. They also promised me their sur-
plus UH-1 helicopter, or "Huey," would be on display by the time this guidebook is published.

Spring Green

Parlor Bar and Grill
101 East Jefferson Street
(608) 588-2363

Spring Green is one of Wisconsin's classiest small communities and deserves a tavern that measures up to community standards. In the Parlor Bar and Grill it's nice to see people get what they deserve. From the canoe paddle door handle on the entrance to the spotless glasses and carefully poured taps, you sense a perfect fit for a folksy and artsy town in the lower Wisconsin River valley.

Some say it is here that you will find the freshest Leinenkugel draft in all of southern Wisconsin. It's no accident, since the Parlor is the proudest booster of the Indian gal label that I encountered in all my tavern tours. Southwest Wisconsin brew partisans needn't worry, New Glarus and Berghoff bottles back up the Leinie's taps.

The Parlor is already a favorite among the tavern touring crowd. Quite a few beer savvy folks make this a pit stop on the run between the brewpubs in Reedsburg and Mineral Point. It is also a natural way-station if you're on a Wisconsin River valley tour from Sauk City to Prairie du Chien. This spot really has the welcome mat out for travelers. No cliques here!

Few taverns have so many great day trip or camping trip tie-ins. Tower Hill State Park, the Springs Resort, American Players Theater, and the Silver Star Inn B and B are only minutes away. Within walking distance are a number of craft shops and studios. Next door is the Gard Theater, which offers a mix of movies, plays, and live music. I'd be remiss if I didn't mention that Spring Green has a bit of a downtown tavern district, with diverse spots that represent at least four different subcultures. A belt of supper clubs on Highway 14 on the north edge of town provides additional imbibing choices.

Oops, almost forgot, the Parlor Bar and Grill also holds its own on sandwiches and appetizers. The menu is not extensive, but it is very well received by the tired and grubby canoeists who trudge in at the end of summer days.

▼ ▼ ▼ ▼ ▼ ▼ ▼ ▼ ▼ ▼ ▼ ▼ ▼ ▼ ▼ ▼ ▼ ▼

Trempealeau Hotel
150 Main Street
(608) 534-6898

Here's another scenic Mississippi River spot that our Gopher neighbors to the west have discovered before the homebred Badgers. And why not? Acts like Arlo Guthrie, Marshall Tucker, Ozark Mountain Daredevils, Floyd Westerman, and Country Joe McDonald will sometimes do an intimate performance here on a Saturday night after playing a big hall in the Twin Cities on Friday.

But if the music is what originally pulls folks in, it's the bar, food, and lodging that keeps them coming back. Leinie's taps keep the locals happy, while bottled Sierra Nevada, Black Dog, Samuel Adams, and Summit selections fill the needs of Minnesotans. About a dozen imports are kept on hand for southern Wisconsinites who happen to stumble in. Tasty appetizers (walnut balls) and desserts (sour cream poppyseed cake and Swedish apple pie) have richly deserved reputations.

This is a place that is classy without being upscale and casually elegant without being prissy. The customer mix is often dictated by music events and the ebb and flow through town. But even jam-packed with brokers, bikers, and bluesmen, it is Wisconsin at its best elbow-rubbing and elbow-bending form.

The Trempealeau Hotel is a perfect end destination or layover spot for a tavern tour. Seven rooms upstairs and a cottage by the river provide comfy lodging. Be advised: this will not be a restful stop for light sleepers or those who go to bed early. Sleeping patterns must be geared to bar hours and freight train schedules. Bring your earplugs.

Northwest Wisconsin

▼ ▼ ▼ ▼ ▼ ▼ ▼ ▼ ▼ ▼ ▼ ▼ ▼ ▼ ▼ ▼ ▼ ▼ ▼

This is wild and woolly tavern territory. The area is flush with lodge-style taverns, old roadhouses, tarpaper-shack beer joints, and lakeside bars. The cities and villages are home to many gritty but friendly taverns in the shadows of warehouses and grain elevators.

Much of the area is hardscrabble country. Farms in the old pine forest area struggle, and in many parts of the region jobs are scarce even in good times. Grassroots groups fight environmental battles with multinational corporations and federal and state agencies.

Many of the rural sections of this area have very low tavern densities. Many two- and three-tavern villages have been reduced to one. In no other area of the state did I experience as much attrition of taverns I had hoped to list.

On the other hand, northwest Wisconsin is rich with scenic beauty and worthy destinations. The Upper Mississippi and St. Croix rivers provide continuation of the Highway 35 tour that begins in southwest Wisconsin and has many quaint river town taverns from Bay City to St. Croix Falls. The Chippewa flowage and Lac Courte Oreilles vicinity have an abundance of vintage resort bars. Highway 13 from west of Stratford to Superior, including the Bayfield to Port Wing loop, offers small town after small town of rustic bars.

The bigger population centers have their own tavern assets. Eau Claire has a bustling downtown tavern district and many respectable neighborhood establishments. Chippewa Falls bears the imprint of the local Leinenkugel brewery and still has a number of unrestored taverns that are prized for their authentic pre–World War II feel. Superior is in a class by itself as a modest-sized city, international port of call, and neighbor to Duluth, Minnesota. The campuses of Menominee and River Falls add youthful spice to the taverns of those two communities.

As for the smaller cities and villages, there are some with notable reputations for tavern hospitality. They may not have all the amenities and options of their urban cousins, but they do score well on the fellowship and fun scale. Worthy of mention are Neillsville, Hudson, Ashland, Spooner, Hayward, and Washburn.

The tiny out-of-the-way places are also worthy of the explorer's time and effort. Small taverns run by folksy eccentrics can be found throughout northwest Wisconsin. Many last only a few seasons before restless owners decide to try their hands at other businesses. Such spots do not lend themselves to guidebook parameters. But I'd be remiss if I didn't leave readers something to discover and claim as their own. Enjoy.

▼ ▼ ▼ ▼ ▼ ▼ ▼ ▼ ▼ ▼ ▼ ▼ ▼ ▼ ▼ ▼ ▼ ▼

Ashland

L.C. Wilmarth's
Deep Water Grill

808 W. Main Street
(715) 682-9199

South Shore Brewery and its on-premises saloons have been a favorite on the brewpub circuit for the last several years. As irreverent as it sounds, a number of friends used it as a way stop after northwoods funerals and many a cheerful toast was offered up to departed fellow beer drinkers. Then, darn it, the brewery and Railyard Pub burned down and left mourners aplenty for its brews.

Like a phoenix from the ashes, South Shore (and the Deep Water Grill) is back and slaking thirst up by the Big Lake. The place still draws from far and wide, with a fan base including locals, seasonal visitors, and upper Great Lakes beer fanciers. The solid reputation of the kettles' content has also survived the fire and relocation.

What's not to like about good beer in this old ore and timber town? Sure, it's a shame that the historic rail connection was lost to the flames. But the whole area lives and breathes the history and lore of the rugged pinery. Mix in the diverse crowd that attends this spot and you won't find it hard to elicit all manner of commentary on lakefaring, logging, fishing, and homesteading after a few brews.

It should be mentioned that serious tavern tourers often use South Shore as the kick-off spot in a circuit known as the "Highway 13 Loop." The particulars vary from group to group, but usually involve extended pubcrawls of Ashland, Washburn, and Bayfield. Those strong of constitution press on to Red Cliff, Herbster, and points west. A few even insist on a return circuit via U.S. Highway 2 and some hidden spots rumored to exist in Brule River country.

▼ ▼ ▼ ▼ ▼ ▼ ▼ ▼ ▼ ▼ ▼ ▼ ▼ ▼ ▼ ▼ ▼ ▼

Bruce

McGinty's Log Bar
Highway 40—Main Street
(715) 868-4635

Don't look for a log building. More than one seeker has been thrown off by this assumption. The exterior blends right into a block of local businesses. The inside is the log lodge. The 1950s vintage log motif runs throughout McGinty's, with a log cabin walk-in cooler, log back bar, and log arches over the restrooms and game room. The contrasts between the standard commercial exterior and Northwoods interior are thrown into further relief by a ceiling covered with carpet square remnants.

It doesn't get much folksier than McGinty's. The bartenders are at ease in modest conversation, and the patrons can regale you with classic Northwoods tales of winter's rigors. One regular likes to poke fun at tipsy snowmobilers and has a repertoire of macabre anecdotes about high-speed encounters with fences and utility poles. One summer seasonal visitor kept our tavern tour entourage in stitches for an hour with his nonstop Ole and Lena jokes in a Norwegian accent.

A visit is instructive about both the sturdiness of the north's small towns and the economic forces and lack of opportunities in rural areas bypassed by tourism. The spot is off the beaten path of today's tourist who is zipping northward to a timeshare or a casino. But there was a time when beat-up boats were towed behind beat-up station wagons, exploring for little-fished lakes and seldom-visited taverns. It's still that sort of place.

The beverage selection is modest: national brands, Milwaukee's Best, Grain Belt, and the Leinie's line. Also, champagne by the bottle! The one-item menu delivers a serviceable homemade hot beef sandwich.

McGinty's is the type of Northwoods tavern that served as the model two generations ago. Now such places are endangered. Visit them while they still exist!

▼ ▼ ▼ ▼ ▼ ▼ ▼ ▼ ▼ ▼ ▼ ▼ ▼ ▼ ▼ ▼ ▼ ▼ ▼

Chippewa Falls

Dam Bar

353 E. Canal Street
(715) 732-9599

No, the name is not an epithet, it's just that the place is near the dam and under the bridge. Many non-locals say this is a harder place to navigate to than the unpaved crossroads in the middle of nowhere that I love to send people to. You can see the tavern from Chippewa Fall's main bridge, but you must backtrack through residential neighborhoods to get there.

As recently as the year 2000 this was known as Bogie's Bar and was one of the livelier blue collar spots in northwest Wisconsin. What was said in the first edition of the guidebook still stands: definitely not a fern bar, good rock-and-roll jukebox, and a nice cross section of locals. The bar surface is still sparkly with embedded coins and seashells.

So the overall mood is much the same. What has changed somewhat are hours and demographics. Weekdays are on a 3 P.M. to close schedule, while on Saturday the doors open at 10 A.M. and Sunday at 6 P.M. Weeknights the crowd seems a little older than the twenty-somethings who hung out here in the 1990s (actually some of the regulars are the same, just chronologically advanced like the rest of us). Some of the working women who hung out here after a shift are now mothers who only get out on weekends.

The crowd does shift toward younger folks on weekends, but not in ways that drive out those from the neighborhood. The conversation here runs a familiar blue collar gamut: sports, music, and outdoors activity. My tavern tour gang ranks it one of their favorite spots to sip a Leinie's.

So even with the name change, there's continuity to be found at the Dam Bar that is ebbing away elsewhere in Chippewa Falls. This area has lost some old classic places in the last decade. More than a few taverns in the Chippewa Valley have shifted to younger crowds or have bit the dust. Nice to see one spot hang in there.

▼ ▼ ▼ ▼ ▼ ▼ ▼ ▼ ▼ ▼ ▼ ▼ ▼ ▼ ▼ ▼

Eau Claire

Northwoods Brew Pub & Grill

3560 Oakwood Mall Drive
(715) 552-0511
www.northwoodsbrewpub.com

Even true-blue bar stool denizens will be tempted to repair to the stuffed chairs in the large space off to the side of the bar. There, a fireplace and warm log walls transport you to that Northwoods lodge all true Wisconsinites have in their mind's eye. During my visit I spotted several patrons reading newspapers and books—a sure sign that customers feel at home.

It's easy to fall into gender-differentiation traps when talking about taverns in general and brew pubs in particular. Even though many women like the brew pub atmosphere, cultural and personal-safety issues often act to discourage women from visting many brew pub sites. That phenomenon is most obvious when the brew pub sits in a dark warehouse district or in an urban core. The Northwoods Brew Pub and Grill location does appeal to women on several counts. The location in a shopping center area makes for easy access and easy parking. Not to mention that it makes a great lunchtime or after-work stop in the midst of errands to bookstores, gift shops, and pharmacies. Patterns of business location have been altered by automobile culture, and here's one bit of evidence that our beer emporiums may undergo that shift, too.

The Northwoods Brew Pub is noted for several distinctive year-round brews. Half Moon Gold is a light-bodied ale. Red Cedar Red measures up as an assertive red. Birch Wood Ale is a milder transition ale for those unaccustomed to full-flavored brews. Poplar Porter has just the right "charred" character. Dark Walnut Stout is a milder but complex stout that wins over non–stout drinkers. Spring brings the addition of Wascally Wheat, while summer heralds Honey Wheat.

The menu sports a large appetizer list (including the mysterious Northwoods Oysters). I can vouch for an excellent French onion ale soup and a hearty wild rice soup. Customers comment favorably on the sandwiches and the dinner menu. The atmosphere, the food, and the brew make Northwoods Brew Pub and Grill a must-stop for those traveling Interstate 94.

▼ ▼ ▼ ▼ ▼ ▼ ▼ ▼ ▼ ▼ ▼ ▼ ▼ ▼ ▼ ▼ ▼ ▼

Grand View
Doug's Grand View Inn
22270 Highway 63
(715) 763-3202

Getting here is half the fun. You could easily use Highway 63 or Highway 13 as your northbound route, depending on which side of the state you're starting from. But give yourself a breather, find Bayfield County M and then County D up through Lake Namekagon country to that blip in the road known as Grand View.

This is one of those classic northwoods taverns that serves as a four-season hub for recreation when weather systems feel like cooperating. One local wag said, "this was a good snowmobilers' bar in the days before global warming." Then the next year dropped two years worth on the area.

It was my good fortune to first visit Doug's under auspicious circumstances and in great company. The occasion was the opening day of bear season, September, 2000 and my companions were Tom Thornton and Butch Tutor, two of Bayfield County's finest sportsmen. They were toasting my luck (in no small part due to their assistance) in harvesting a 350 pound black bear on my first hunt. Believe me, that is a circumstance that will imprint a tavern on you for the rest of your days.

That is the stuff of memories of a tavern in the north country. The monster muskies landed, the big bucks that got away, and the haunting call of the loon are inextricably bound up with those waterholes we repair to after such brushes with Mother Nature. Then the place becomes part of our personal narrative and if we're lucky we'll number sufficient days longevity to bring another generation around and regale them with stories of "back then."

When you bring them into Doug's you'll have the whole Leinie's line to choose from (in bottles). There's also pizza, burgers, Friday fish fry, broasted chicken, and Saturday prime rib. Heck, you might even run into Tom and Butch.

▼ ▼ ▼ ▼ ▼ ▼ ▼ ▼ ▼ ▼ ▼ ▼ ▼ ▼ ▼ ▼ ▼

ANOTHER ROUND

More Boyer Beer Favorites

Best Farm Country Tour: Riley Tavern (Verona), Hooterville Inn (Blue Mounds), Lucky's (Barneveld), Hyde Store (north of Ridgeway), and Pleasant Ridge Store (north of Dodgeville)

Best Mid-State Tour: Holly Rocks (Wisconsin Rapids), Witz End (Stevens Point), Northland Ballroom (Rosholt-Iola), Virgie Hunter's (rural Mosinee), and Scott Street Pub (Wausau).

Best Day in the Big City: Pub crawl of Water Street, Old World Third Street, and South Second in Milwaukee.

Best Neighborhood Pub Crawl: Madison near east side (Williamson Street, Atwood Avenue, and Winnebago Street).

Best Day in Lake Superior: South Shore Brewery (Ashland), pub crawl of Washburn, pub crawl of Bayfield, and Tom's Burnt Down Cafe (Madeline Island).

Best Tavern Tour: An adaptation of the Great River Road along the Mississippi, starting at Potosi, continuing northward through Cassville, Bloomington, Prairie du Chien, Ferryville, Stoddard, LaCrosse, Trempealeau, Fountain City, Bay City, Prescott, River Falls, Hudson, and St. Croix Falls. Give yourself a week.

▼ ▼ ▼ ▼ ▼ ▼ ▼ ▼ ▼ ▼ ▼ ▼ ▼ ▼ ▼ ▼ ▼ ▼

Hayward
Moccasin Bar and Northwoods Wildlife Museum
15806 1st Street (at Highways 27 and 63)
(715) 634-4211

Hold onto your hats here! The angle of this joint is as subtle as a two-by-four between the eyes. I'd be the first to admit that many of my referrals in this guidebook are based on nuances that are seldom detected in the casual one-stop. Even if your hearing isn't what it used to be, your bifocals call out the need to go trifocal, and your regard for popular culture begins and ends with Monday Night Football, you'll "get it" at the Moccasin Bar. Here you won't need the folklorist's persistence to bag an authentic tall tale. Such legends are dripping off the walls.

Moccasin Bar approaches its task with tongue firmly in cheek. The bar is a fun spot, and its "museum" display cases are a hoot. The P. T. Barnum tradition is alive and well with oddities, straightforward trophies, and thigh-slappers among the exhibits. On the one hand are items like the largest mounted muskie, albino mammals, owls, and commemorative rifles. On the other hand are bizarre stuffed-animal scenes, with raccoons bedecked in jewelry and foxes in courtrooms. In between you will find real-life accounts of renowned fishing guides and epic man-versus-fish struggles in framed clippings.

The displays guarantee a constant stream of visitors that include vanloads of children, grandmothers in walkers, and gawking city folk. The fishermen and duck hunters sit at the bar while the music blares. Throw in a bank of video games and two pool tables and you end up with a bazaar of sights and sounds. Part of the crowd spills over from the attached *Northern Exposure*–style eatery called the Moose Cafe.

You won't find a busier bar on a Sunday morning, although it's lively the rest of the week, too. Regulars stop in for the standard national draft beer on tap. Those of us passing through favor the Leinie's line in bottles. Hard-core sportsmen feast on bar sandwiches and pizzas, but most patrons eat first at the Moose Cafe. The local ritual involves a "shake" of the dice and a $1 mystery shot.

▼ ▼ ▼ ▼ ▼ ▼ ▼ ▼ ▼ ▼ ▼ ▼ ▼ ▼ ▼ ▼ ▼ ▼

Hudson

Barker's Bar and Grill

413 2nd Street

(715) 386-4123

www.barkerbarandgrill.com

R eaders must be warned that this entry is my way of sneaking in another bar on the Great Tavern Road, otherwise known as Highway 35 or the Great River Road. Some purists might insist that fresh-ground Guatemalan coffee, homemade *pico de gallo* salsa, and a zillion appetizers on a well-stocked menu moves Barker's out of the tavern category. But I would never pass up a place just because it has a daylong flow of sit-down and take-out food customers. The Neanderthals will just have to find their beef jerky, pickled eggs, and generic canned beer elsewhere.

Yes, it is a bar, has a bar to sit at, and has regulars who visit daily for beer. Yes, plenty of beer: 17 taps and 14 bottled brands. Lots of turnover here and local requests. During my fall 1998 visit, a popular draft was St. Croix Maple Ale, and the bartop sported plenty of Moosehead bottles.

And good beer conversation. The regulars include a number of folks who travel far and wide on the brew pub circuit and like to drop in on the microbreweries when they can. This makes for some darn good leads to other nearby towns. Their knowledge base is also extensive about the neighboring watering holes in Minnesota. Here the true-blue brew fans come out before dark, so, unlike in many of my favorite spots, you can sample St. Croix hospitality before the day slips away.

Those expecting a "Northwoods" tavern might be disappointed, though I'd wager they'll get over it real quick. The open "kitchen" behind the bar gives Barker's a snazzy modern diner feel that pulls in Minnesotans and others with tavern phobias. Smoking is not prohibited but is definitely discouraged. A screened deck out back makes for pleasant early evening sipping in summer.

▼ ▼ ▼ ▼ ▼ ▼ ▼ ▼ ▼ ▼ ▼ ▼ ▼ ▼ ▼ ▼ ▼ ▼ ▼

Tom's Burned Down Cafe
Highway H
(715) 747-6100

Many readers of the first edition of this guide thought that the previous entry on this establishment was my form of a "gotcha." Some complained that "there's no there, there." Well, I wouldn't go that far. There are few watering holes this side of the tropics with such a distinctive sense of place.

So what if I neglected to mention that Tom's lacks a building per se? Well, it does have a mobile home or construction trailer that houses restrooms. And there are a few plank walls beneath the awnings, tarps, and tentage. By now you get the picture, this is a warm season spot. So my initial caution stands, call before you take that Madeline Island ferry out from Bayfield.

The first edition's vague depiction was not an effort to play cute. It was more of a concern that readers might not believe an accurate narrative. Since then my tavern depictions in *Cream City Suds* have proven that I don't make this stuff up.

A review of the place might focus on the salvage sculpture guarding the place. Or it could hone in on a sensibility that one local wag described as "redneck/bohemian/punk." It might even call attention to middle-aged interlopers wolfing pizzas and downing Leinie's at the plank bar. Let it suffice to describe the panorama of one summer eve's visit: a jazz tuba soloist, a conga line of anti-mining activists, a heated non-verbal argument with a mime, and an old geezer dancing the twist on a table with a multi-pierced goth chick. Phase of the moon or was David Lynch filming nearby? I'll never tell, go check it out for yourself.

▼ ▼ ▼ ▼ ▼ ▼ ▼ ▼ ▼ ▼ ▼ ▼ ▼ ▼ ▼ ▼ ▼

Menomonie

The Buck
315 Main Street
(715) 235-9390

A play on words creates lighthearted confusion at the site of the Silver Dollar Saloon and Brick Company. "The Buck" was appended to the bar area of this business as shorthand for the basic unit of U.S. currency. The overall establishment and dining area are given the longer appellation. This is a favorite spot for tavern lovers in northwest Wisconsin. When you ask the sales reps and beer distributors in the area which bar they like, many shoot back "the Buck" as fast as a pool table break shot.

A classic rock CD collection (with plenty of Eric Clapton) keeps the Buck at a high energy level. If you have a hankering for a sandwich or dinner, you might want to relocate to the dining areas. The food is well regarded by some of my trustier sources. On Friday afternoons there is a pleasant Cheers-type ambience. A healthy mix of UW-Stout students, downtown professionals, and blue-collar beer purists are drawn by the 20 import beers and Guinness and New Glarus brews on tap. The full Leinie's line finds favor here, with Leinenkugel's Creamy Draft filling a comfortable niche. The Buck's Bloody Mary is a favorite in Menominee.

Many taverns sponsor sports teams. More than a few take pride in those teams and the trophies they bring home to roost behind the bar. These sports enthusiasts take a backseat to no one in that regard, with team spirit that extends year-round. The crowd at the Buck takes this competitive spirit a step further with a widely appreciated cheerleading squad.

This crowd also excels in another area: that of Minnesota humor. Well, some of it is humor. Some of it must be labeled as creative insult. A tinier category might fall within the realm of defamation if those stolid Minnesotans were prone to litigation. On my last visit the barrage was directed at Vikings, Gophers, and the Mall of America. Where Garrison Keillor uses the wry approach, Buck denizens use wisecracking smart bombs.

▼ ▼ ▼ ▼ ▼ ▼ ▼ ▼ ▼ ▼ ▼ ▼ ▼ ▼ ▼ ▼ ▼

Minong
Fluffy's Corner Bar
203 Fifth Avenue
(715) 466-4318

Fluffy's was a totally accidental find. Visits to other area taverns brought warnings to avoid Fluffy's and vague complaints about "that wild place" from elderly patrons of more sedate spots. The red flags, of course, whetted my desire to check it out.

What I found was part Northwoods tavern, part Harley-Davidson biker bar, and part town hall. During the day it's pretty much a family place. By evening it's decidedly adult. Delicate souls are forewarned about off-color signs and "art." Meat Loaf seems to be a favorite on the jukebox. Customers sometimes yell conversations down the length of the bar. But you know, it's a friendly place. It's the tavern equivalent of a well-broken-in work boot: scuffed and not much to look at, but comfortable as all get-out.

No one knows for sure what beers are available in Fluffy's. It seems to depend on who asks. Sure, the standard brands are all represented. But the quick eye will pick up furtive bartender moves to pluck Guinness Stout, Heineken, and other unheralded exotic fare from the cooler depths. One patron offered the theory that any beer sold in Big T's, an adjoining business connected by a low doorway, might show up in Fluffy's. My companion and I tested the proposition and found a bit of sweet talk did indeed produce results.

Fluffy's has its share of physically imposing customers, often in leather with Harley logos. Yet they are full of pleasant surprises, as I found when one grizzled biker made an on-the-money referral to a great prime rib supper club and allowed that the red meat was accompanied by the Northwoods' best cabernet list. But he was one of those quirky types that show up in places like this—filled with Beat generation literary references and spouting quotes from the works of eco-renegade Edward Abbey.

ANOTHER ROUND

Some Wisconsin Beer Facts

First Commercial Brewery: Phillips Brewery in Mineral Point, founded in 1835. This business evolved into the Mineral Springs Brewery, which continued brewing until 1961. Wisconsin's second brewery, Rablin & Bray, opened in 1836 in an abandoned Black Hawk War log fort at Elk Grove, Lafayette County.

Most Durable Brewery: Joseph Huber in Monroe. Despite many restructurings and name changes, this brewery traces its roots back to 1848. It continues to offer beer under the Huber and Berghoff labels.

Old and New Styles: G. Heileman's initial main brand was Gold Leaf Beer. It was replaced in 1902 by Old Style Lager. The new brew acquired an excellent word-of-mouth reputation. In 1933, when Prohibition was repealed, the reopened brewery worked around the clock to fill back orders from places as distant as Los Angeles and the West Indies. A riot nearly broke out when caravans of truckers descended on La Crosse and refused to leave town without full loads of beer.

▼ ▼ ▼ ▼ ▼ ▼ ▼ ▼ ▼ ▼ ▼ ▼ ▼ ▼ ▼ ▼ ▼

Neillsville
Green Lantern
231 W. Seventh Street
(715) 743-3663

Neillsville is one of those towns where one of its eight or nine taverns always seems to be reopening, shutting down, or changing hands. Tavern culture is lively here (much like Ridgeway and Hollandale down in my Iowa County turf) and reminiscent of the old-fashioned shot-and-a-beer ethic. Several of the local spots are high-octane testosterone bars, featuring nude calendars and (mostly) good-natured profanity.

Such tavern-blessed towns usually have at least one bar that takes a lower-key approach. But nearly 20 years of stopping in Neillsville for a quick one (OK, a quick two) kept me in a one- or two-block area of reliable (as in open for business) taverns. Then came the revelation. It came in strange form, too, for someone accustomed to hearing tales in tavern settings. Instead, I went to a sacred place to hear a strange tale and as a bonus was steered to an unassuming place called the Green Lanern.

The Green Lantern stands apart from the other bars, a bit quieter and more reflective, and set off a bit from the main tavern cluster. It is not uncommon to run into visitors and staff from the Highground, Wisconsin's Vietnam Veterans Memorial. Don't worry, you won't be a captive audience for someone else's war stories. But you just might get to eavesdrop on middle-aged men in fatigues whispering about a youth spent in a faraway land. On rainy days campers and fishermen stop by to dry out, wet the whistle, and plug a jukebox that carries polkas and Jim Morrison.

Simplicity is the password here, with only two beer taps—both Old Milwaukee. Cans and bottles: if it's not Miller or Old Style, it's exotic. Liquor: only what regular customers ask for (and don't expect anything with fruit or tiny umbrellas). Food: burger, fish sandwich, chicken sandwich, and fish fry ($4.25!). Be nice to Rosie behind the bar and she might give you a bowl of peanuts in the shell. If you're up after the big buck, she can also get you a range pass for the Neillsville Gun Club.

▼ ▼ ▼ ▼ ▼ ▼ ▼ ▼ ▼ ▼ ▼ ▼ ▼ ▼ ▼ ▼ ▼ ▼ ▼

River Falls

Main Streeter Bar and Grill
212 S. Main Street
(715) 425-2202

Here's a watering hole with a brand-spanking-new look that nevertheless possesses character and holds a crowd of regulars. This is one of the most family-friendly taverns I encountered in my travels. Plenty of video games for the kids and an endless supply of popcorn. The Main Streeter is a favorite of parents visiting UW–River Falls and also picks up quite a few day-trippers from Minnesota. All mingle at the bar and exchange sports talk and local news. The place has a pleasant buzz and smiling faces, not the high-decibel roar or the sullen silence that you find in some spots.

Ten taps tell the tale of draft beer for thirsty crowds, with Leinie's, the nationals, and Pete's Wicked Ale. The coolers usually hold 25 different bottled beers, including the full Leinie's line and a few rarities like Newcastle Brown Ale. If you hit the place at the right time you're likely to hear young faculty arguing with gray-templed carpenters about macrobrews versus microbrews. The surprise is in who takes which side.

A diverse crowd hints at the Main Streeter's triple duty as sports bar, downtown lunch spot, and 30-something meeting place. The menu bucks Wisconsin tradition by not offering a fish fry. The top food item is a very good half-pound burger. Regular patrons also vouch for the other sandwiches and daily specials. It's a testament to the atmosphere and offerings that so many travelers become repeat customers. One elderly woman from Eau Claire told me this is one of only three taverns she would set foot in.

The Main Streeter probably represents a sturdy middle ground for the taverns of the future, outside of the emerging franchise operations. Not all will be able to go glitzy, pull in the bands, or set up brewing operations. Some, like this one, will carve out a niche as modernized family taverns that make everyone feel welcome.

▼ ▼ ▼ ▼ ▼ ▼ ▼ ▼ ▼ ▼ ▼ ▼ ▼ ▼ ▼ ▼ ▼ ▼ ▼

Solon Springs

Village Pump
11575 South Business 53
(715) 378-2212

T his is the party spot for the surrounding area. Even on a Saturday night you might well end up in the middle of someone's birthday celebration, anniversary party, or wedding reception (I put $5 in a pitcher to dance with a new bride). The large, open lodge-style construction makes this one of the biggest tavern venues north of Eau Claire. A long bar means that there is rarely a stool shortage.

Regular customers like their draft beer, even though the four tap selections are limited to standard national brands. Leinie's and a few imports are available in bottles. Local quirks include demand for Busch Light in bottles and Leinie's in cans. The regulars also go through a lot of brandy. One trusty source told me that at least one segment of the crowd here likes to play drinking games, though that pursuit seemed to be the province of the younger folks.

The regulars like to shoot pool and play cards. During one visit I ran into a wedding rehearsal party, and the bride was shooting pool with her veil on. We were told that they host quite a few bachelor and bachelorette parties where the revelers shoot pool throughout the event, except when one of the participants ends up dancing on the table. As with many small-town events, the general public is welcome, no matter if the occasion is Johnny's welcome back from boot camp or Grandma and Grandpa's anniversary.

The Village Pump is geared mainly to the younger, active crowd. There is a high turnover at the bar stools, with 20-somethings in and out for quick burgers and beer. So it's not a place for prolonged conversation, but you can catch the buzz about what's going on locally and track down the four-season recreational opportunities that abound in the area. The jukebox is well stocked and people dance to it, even to sad Patsy Cline numbers.

Some would say that the Village Pump represents an updating of the roadhouse-style tavern, and they'd be part right. The layout is reminiscent of many roadhouse variations and certainly holds its own on floor space with the heftier representatives of that species. What is different is the brighter and airier interior and the clearer demarcations between the spaces devoted to different recreational purposes. It took a bit of getting used to, but I can now see that they planned wisely. They just might have come up with a new model.

▼ ▼ ▼ ▼ ▼ ▼ ▼ ▼ ▼ ▼ ▼ ▼ ▼ ▼ ▼ ▼ ▼ ▼

St. Croix Falls

Kassel Tap Bar
Highways 8 and 35 North
(715) 483-9390

K assel's, as many of the locals refer to it, has been in its current incarnation for about 15 years. Because a number of predecessor bars operated on this site, there are three and four generations of some outdoors families with a tradition of using this spot as a way station for their trips "up north." One of the best things that can happen to a first-time visitor is for one of the elderly gentlemen who still drop in here to regale them with his memories of fishing and hunting trips his father took him on and how those trips included a boy's first tavern visit.

Memories of rites of passage hang as thick around the white heads of those old-timers as smoke from a pipe. First muskie caught on a hand-carved lure. First overnight canoe passage on an isolated flowage in a custom-crafted cedar canoe. First big buck in a camp of skilled hunters who had waited decades for a trophy. First beer in a bar with Dad and the uncles. So at its best, Kassel's is primed for memories of the Wisconsin that no longer exists.

But don't tell that to the regulars. Many of them consider it a combination outdoorsmen's and sports bar. It's considered the local spot to catch big games on the bar TV. Locals, hunters, fishermen, and vacationers mingle here. In summers, softball teams stop by to quench their thirst while volleyball teams work up a thirst on the courts out back. Road construction crews also seem to be among the perennial visitors.

The three taps and bottled beers are limited to the standard nationals and Northwoods regionals, which is just fine for the blue-collar regulars. Others opt for the hot beef sandwiches and pickled asparagus (sold in jars to go as well). Polk County friends swear that Kassel Tap is the political and social barometer for the area, with frequent animated conversations on land use topics. When they're talking politics in here, they're talking conservation from the pre–ecology movement perspective.

ANOTHER ROUND

Wisconsin Brew Pubs

Be sure to call ahead for the hours each is open.

Angelic Brewing Company
322 West Johnson Street
Madison
(608) 257-2707
www.angelicbrewing.com

Appleton Brewing Company
1004 S. Olde Oneida Street
Appleton
(920) 731-3322

Brewery Creek Inn and Pub
23 Commerce Street
Mineral Point
(608) 987-3298
www.brewerycreek.com
(See page 60 for full description.)

Brewmasters Brew Pub and Brewmasters Northside
4017 80th Street and 1170 22nd Avenue
Kenosha
(262) 694-9050 and (262) 552-2085
(See page 13 for full description.)

Brown Street Brewery
16 North Brown Street
Rhinelander
(715) 369-2100

Delafield Brewhaus
3832 Hillside Drive
Delafield
(262) 646-7821

▼ ▼ ▼ ▼ ▼ ▼ ▼ ▼ ▼ ▼ ▼ ▼ ▼ ▼ ▼ ▼ ▼ ▼

Fox River Brewing Company
1501 Arboretum Drive
Oshkosh
(920) 232-2337

Fox River Brewing Company (No. 2)
4301 Wisconsin Avenue
Appleton
(920) 991-0000

Great Dane Pub and Brewing Company
123 E. Doty Street
Madison
(608) 284-0000
www.greatdanepub.com

Grumpy Troll Brew Pub
105 S. Second Street
Mount Horeb
(608) 437-2739
(See page 36 for full description.)

J. T. Whitney's Brewpub
674 S. Whitney Way
Madison
(608) 274-1776
www.jtwhitneys.com

Milwaukee Ale House
233 N. Water Street
Milwaukee
(414) 226-2337
www.ale-house.com
(See page 30 for full description.)

Minocqua Brewing Company
238 Lake Shore Drive
Minocqua
(715) 358-3040
www.minocquabrewingco.com

Moosejaw Pizza & Brewing Company
110 Wisconsin Dells Parkway South
Wisconsin Dells
(608) 253-4687

▼ ▼ ▼ ▼ ▼ ▼ ▼ ▼ ▼ ▼ ▼ ▼ ▼ ▼ ▼ ▼ ▼ ▼ ▼

Northwoods Brew Pub and Grill
3560 Oakwood Mall Drive
Eau Claire
(715) 552-0511
www.northwoodsbrewpub.com
(See page 82 for full description.)

Rail House Brewing Company
W1130 Old Peshtigo Road
Marinette
(715) 732-4646
(See page 112 for full description.)

Randy's Fun Hunters Brewery
841 E. Milwaukee Street
Whitewater
(262) 473-8000
(See page 48 for full description.)

Rock Bottom Brewery
740 N. Plankinton Road
Milwaukee
(414) 276-3030

Rowland's Calumet Brewing Company
25 N. Madison Street
Chilton
(920) 849-2534
(See page 6 for full description.)

Shipwrecked Brewpub
7791 Egg Harbor Road
Egg Harbor
(920) 868-2767

South Shore Brewery
808 W. Main Street
Ashland
(715) 682-9199

Titletown Brewery
200 Douseman Street
Green Bay
(920) 437-2337
www.titletownbrewery.com

▼ ▼ ▼ ▼ ▼ ▼ ▼ ▼ ▼ ▼ ▼ ▼ ▼ ▼ ▼ ▼ ▼ ▼

Water Street Brewery
1101 N. Water Street
Milwaukee
(414) 272-1195
www.waterstreetbrewery.com
(See page 34 for full description.)

Water Street Brewery Lake Country
3191 Golf Road
Delafield
(262) 646-7878

▼ ▼ ▼ ▼ ▼ ▼ ▼ ▼ ▼ ▼ ▼ ▼ ▼ ▼ ▼ ▼ ▼

Superior
Anchor Bar and Grill
413 Tower Avenue
(715) 394-9747

Not much to look at from the outside, and located in a gritty warehouse neighborhood, "Da Anchor" (as many locals refer to it) is a delight to enter and survey. My referral source spoke of its "maritime look" and conjured up an image of tavern à la Red Lobster. What a misimpression!

The interior could be the cove-side cottage of an old salt. It is as if a massive northeaster blew all the flotsam and jetsam between Nova Scotia and Isle Royale right through the Anchor's front door. The result is an eclectic but warm beachcomber's clutter. The late-Saturday-night crowd I found there was an appropriate mix of blue-collar, white-collar, students, and down-and-outers, with a sprinkling of merchant seamen.

If you are alone you might be able to find a stool at the short (and usually crowded) bar and pick up on a lively conversation. A weathered old chap told me an eerie haunted lighthouse tale. He put a whole new light on the sweeping beam that peeked through the motor home's windows later that night.

This is the type of place where you don't really need a local character to tell you a story. Da Anchor births them and inspires them. A few hours on the stools and a landlocked flatlander will be spinning yarns before the mast. Good company, heads nodding in encouragement, and good beer see to that. B. Traven, early-twentieth-century writer of a haunting and scathing maritime novel called *Death Ship*, would blend right in here.

But if you are part of a group—especially a hungry group—you are well advised to claim a worn wooden table in one of the book-lined alcoves. While my arrival was not well timed to test the kitchen's mettle, patrons made sure that I knew that *Northland Reader* of Duluth, Minnesota, gave the Anchor its 1998 "Best Really Cheap Eats" award for the Lake Superior country. Hearty and ample characterize the testimonials of regulars I talked to.

The Anchor is the best of a covey of other small but interesting bars in this commercial area. What sets it apart (aside from atmosphere and grub) are the beers. It has a growing collection of bottled micros (15). Space limits it to three tap heads, with a regional and a micro in the rotation. We lucked out with a Lake Superior India Pale Ale.

▼ ▼ ▼ ▼ ▼ ▼ ▼ ▼ ▼ ▼ ▼ ▼ ▼ ▼ ▼ ▼ ▼

Superior

Twin Ports Brewing Company
1623 Broadway
(715) 394-2500
www.twinportsbrewing.com

My trail to this spot took me through a veritable tavern graveyard of beloved joints which had folded or changed beyond recognition. When Big John and I went on the road in the motorhome we thought we'd visit Thunder Road in Eau Claire. We expected to have a beer at Mr. C's in Chippewa Falls and a brandy at the Hogs Head in Spooner. Alas, we could not find a pulse in those quarters.

So up to Superior we went to revisit the Choo-Choo Bar and Grill. Holy lake trout, that was gone too! But here we found a happy ending to the tavern tale. It turns out that the Choo-Choo morphed into Twin Ports Brewing, outgrew the old space, and moved into the old creamery building that currently houses them. The account of the evolution is more complicated than space permits, but suffice it to say there are tales of brewmania to be heard here. If you want the full account you'll just have to visit on your own.

Rick and Nancy Sauer are the beloved hosts of this brewpub. Some see them as a younger version of the Rowlands in Chilton. Rick gained his brewing spurs at the Railhouse in Marinette. They have created a great atmosphere to go with their brews.

Speaking of brews, they manage a nice variety here. At our last inspection we found North Coast Amber Ale, Derailed Ale, Burntwood Black Ale, and Hopfenkopf (hophead). Good stuff! We were told that the future would bring brown ale, imperial Stout, and rye bock.

Northeast Wisconsin

Great Wisconsin Taverns

▼ ▼ ▼ ▼ ▼ ▼ ▼ ▼ ▼ ▼ ▼ ▼ ▼ ▼ ▼ ▼ ▼ ▼

T his diverse area presents many faces, moods, and settings. It is home to isolated lake and loon country and some of Wisconsin's worst sprawl. It is potato farming, forest products, and papermaking. It is prosperity, skilled industrial workers, real estate speculation, and rural poverty. It is an ethnic stew where the original Menominee, Potawatomi, and Ojibwa were joined by French, New England Yankees, displaced eastern tribes, Belgians, Bohemians, Icelanders, Danes, Dutch, Poles, Finns, Norwegians, Swedes, and Germans.

This quadrant of Wisconsin slices across several bioregions and economic clusters. Door County has much in common with the smaller Lake Michigan shore communities stretching into the southeast. Green Bay and Appleton are logically part of the urban belt in the Fox Valley. Sections of national forest lands are indistinguishable from adjacent tracts in the northwest. And while the northeast claims a large chunk of the central sands country, the ancient lake bottom is really part of all four quadrants of the state.

Socially and politically, this is Wisconsin's most conservative region. But it has little of the "dry" tradition of southwest Wisconsin. The landscape is dotted with Catholic and Lutheran churches, often at crossroads with a tavern. The urban portions are noted for hardworking early risers, yet one readily notices more strip joints, in the form of "gentlemen's clubs," than elsewhere in the state.

It is the part of Wisconsin most content to constantly reinvent itself. Despite a proud history that reaches back to the French explorers, the taverns are generally not historic buildings. Some say that the forests in the Northwoods portion, like Yucatan jungles, devour the isolated taverns. In the urban area, bulldozers clean the slate of old neighborhoods and factories to make way for malls. Franchise and chain pubs prove to be very popular.

Still, there are many worthy taverns in the northeast. Backroad searches turn up hidden gems. Resort areas are joining the brew pub and microbrew trend. The cities have many unheralded neighborhood taverns that are 100% pure cheesehead territory. Part of the fun is finding your own favorites and telling other people about them.

▼ ▼ ▼ ▼ ▼ ▼ ▼ ▼ ▼ ▼ ▼ ▼ ▼ ▼ ▼ ▼ ▼ ▼

Algoma

Hudson's Bar and Grill
205 Navarino Street
(920) 487-5493

Hudson's is set up more like a supper club than a bar and grill. Yet it earns the right to belong to the tavern fraternity by providing a comfortable bar and bartenders who treat their domain as more than a brief stop for patrons on the way to the dining area. It also provides one of the great tavern experiences of the Lake Michigan shoreline.

Two short blocks from the lake, gulls often circle nearby. Many customers stroll up from the Algoma boardwalk. Others stop in after tours of the nearby Von Stiehl Winery. In the warmer months it is an ideal place to catch up with the latest lake fishing reports. My introduction to Hudson's came through friends who routinely bring their lake trout and salmon fishing gangs to tell lies after their charter trips.

The taps are from the ranks of the standard nationals, but the bottled selection usually includes regional craft brews. If you like fish with your beer, you're in luck: seaburger, perchburger (a treat), cod, redfish, whitefish, rainbow trout, haddock, pollock, and the local favorite, lake perch. Steaks and hamburgers are available for landlubbers.

Hudson's is also a hit with retired patrons. Many taverns have displaced elderly customers with loud music, foul language, and rowdy 20-somethings chugging six-packs. Management here seems to have come down on the side of the more mature beer drinker and multigenerational family groups that come in for food. Some tavern owners say that such a business can't survive. In Algoma it thrives.

From the Wisconsin heritage perspective, this spot also scores points with those who wish to hear lake yarns, especially about the old sailing-ship days. In each one of my three visits I picked up tales of shipwrecks, lost sailors, and haunted lighthouses. There are, of course, lighthearted stories to be told, too. My favorite was about the old bawdy house that flew various undergarments from its tall flagpole as a signal to passing vessels about which working gals were on duty.

That tale brought denials from women patrons that any such institution had plied sordid trades in Algoma. A grizzled boat repairman said he heard it from his sainted grandfather. Who would argue with that?

▼ ▼ ▼ ▼ ▼ ▼ ▼ ▼ ▼ ▼ ▼ ▼ ▼ ▼ ▼ ▼ ▼ ▼

Appleton

Adler Brau Restaurant and Pub

1004 South Olde Oneida Street
(920) 380-BEER

Here's the online and on-site alternative to mail order beer clubs. It pulls loyal locals and travelers in to sample from 12 award-winning brews produced on the premises. Then it sets customers up to order via the internet. Email them at appbrau@vbe.com and they'll zip back an order form.

The restaurant side of the establishment also gets good reviews. The menu presents numerous choices with its American, German, Italian, and Mexican specialties. The building is almost as old as the state and started as—surprise, surprise—a brewery. This is an excellent alternative to the student hustle and bustle on College Avenue.

The place gets my vote as the best watering hole in Appleton for good conversation, especially if your interests range beyond the Packers. Not that they don't talk sports here; you'll even encounter fans of minor league baseball reliving the feats of the boys of summer. What is more astounding is that you might even hear a rational political discussion here. Elsewhere in town there are those who toast Tailgunner Joe McCarthy and speculate on the positive nutritional value of PCBs.

This brew spot is also to be commended for its bucking of Fox Valley trends toward the strip malling of all cultural institutions. Yes, there is value in preservation. Yes, beer can be joyfully consumed without high-volume TV accompaniment. Yes, there is life after 30.

▼ ▼ ▼ ▼ ▼ ▼ ▼ ▼ ▼ ▼ ▼ ▼ ▼ ▼ ▼ ▼ ▼ ▼

Appleton
Bazil's Pub
109 West College Avenue
(920) 954-1707

Appleton's College Avenue is one of Wisconsin's longest bar strips. Many fine drinking establishments line this heavily commercial thoroughfare. They range from the bars of the young, upscale downtown crowd to the blue-collar shot joints further west. Bazil's Pub bridges those two worlds with a large beer collection.

This party hearty location runs ten taps. It does something different with its taps than most microbrew bars. Instead of going for a variety of brands from different breweries, it'll often run a featured brewery and offer most, if not all, of the available brews from that source. It might offer four or five Gray's at a time, or the local Adler Brau line.

The bottled beer inventory is in the 100 brew range, with heavy import and micro representation. Bazil's also has an extensive menu, with good sandwiches and variations on the usual fried appetizers, like calamari. The diverse crowd also has better gender balance than in most bars. The women regulars appreciate the less-male-dominated atmosphere and the clean facilities.

It's an all-around decent place for any part of the day or any day of the week. Despite its catering to a crowd in their 20s and 30s, those of us in the neighborhood of the big 5-0 are not made to feel like lepers. Service is excellent for a casual dining and drinking spot. Elsewhere on College Avenue the hired help can run toward the sassy side and the bartenders know more about flushing beer than tapping it.

Mere niceness rarely elevates a pub into respectable beer-drinking territory, but it sure doesn't hurt when you have the other qualities that bring people into Bazil's. It's a place that knows how to keep them coming back.

If Bazil's is insufficiently gritty for you, just work your way west on College Avenue. Eventually you'll happen upon the American Legion Club. If the moon is full you just might hear a strange Joe McCarthy story.

▼ ▼ ▼ ▼ ▼ ▼ ▼ ▼ ▼ ▼ ▼ ▼ ▼ ▼ ▼ ▼ ▼ ▼

Appleton

Emmett's Bar & Grill

139 N. Richmond Street

(920) 733-7649

F ox Valley fans of blues and brew were unmerciful in their assessment of my upbringing and character when the first edition of this guide failed to list Emmett's. Truth be known, I did not omit it, I simply missed it in all my years of convention weekends and conferences in Appleton.

This is, for those encroaching on middle age (or well into it), the perfect alternative to youth orientated bars of College Avenue. It has a good age mix most nights, though weekend music can shift the crowd one way or the other. It is a good spot to learn about the music scene in the Fox Valley area.

The ten-tap lineup varies from time to time. On my last visit they were offering Leinies, Sprecher, Guinness, Bass, New Castle Brown, and some of the national big boys. A busy bartender guessed they had about twenty types of bottled beer.

Emmett's is not a large space for music and dancing. It has a wrap-around spatial arrangement that creates a blind spot in terms of crowd watching. The crowd is lively to watch and fairly friendly to new faces. The regulars come to have a good time.

Two of my best evenings out in the last year came at this spot, catching a group called Blue Olives one time and the highway groove of the Dave Steffen Band on another occasion. Then there's bartender Wendy who makes things rock behind the bar.

▼ ▼ ▼ ▼ ▼ ▼ ▼ ▼ ▼ ▼ ▼ ▼ ▼ ▼ ▼ ▼ ▼ ▼

Boulder Junction
Boulder Beer Bar
Highway K and Main Street
(715) 385-2749

Many Wisconsin taverns lay claim to having the most beers available for sale. Behind the inflated rhetoric, inquiring customers hear a lot of "We're temporarily out of . . ." or "The day person must have moved our . . ." You won't hear these excuses at the Boulder Beer Bar. At last count it was at 384 types of bottled beer. Its goal is 500. By all indications it satisfies its claims and will meet its target.

The full line of Wisconsin microbrews from New Glarus, Hinterland, and Wisconsin Brewing are available. All the other Badger State microbreweries are represented by their generally distributed brews. Dozens and dozens of American microbrews also grace the coolers of the Boulder Beer Bar. So do dozens and dozens of quality imports. For example, they carry seven Belgian brews. Europe is very well represented, as are all the other continents with breweries.

One problem associated with a wide selection (aside from bogus claims) is stale and skunky beer. Even bars in large metropolitan areas have slow turnover among more obscure brews. Boulder Beer Bar works to control such difficulties by maintaining small-quantity inventories with a computer system that prompts constant fresh orders.

Boulder Beer Bar is also one of the state's leading snowmobiler bars. It is conveniently located near the heart of the Minoqua–Boulder Junction network of hundreds of miles of snowmobile trails. It is a very lively place in January and February if the white stuff is on the trails. But it's definitely worth a stop in any season. Call ahead for hours. They close some weekdays.

This probably is as good a time as any to figuratively shake the collars of all those sourpusses who possess tavern licenses in this beautiful but beer-deprived corner of Wisconsin. Visit the Boulder Beer Bar! See customers with functioning pulses! Learn that there is more to beer slinging than Schiltz and Pabst! If we can elevate those dreary little wayside bars, with their depressing interiors that draw more on the tradition of the tarpaper shack than the Northwoods lodge, to one-tenth of the ambition of the Boulder Beer Bar, well, we will have ourselves a renaissance.

Bowler

Starlight Bar
(in the North Star Casino)
Hwy A
(715) 787-3110

Drinking beer or other alcoholic beverages is not what brings most patrons into the complex owned and operated by the Mohican band of Stockbridge-Munsee in northwest Shawano County. But unlike a lot of casino bars, this bar holds its own in business. Sometimes it's like its own little community within the casino. Casino crowds are weighted heavily toward seniors, but here at the bar is where you're most likely to meet people who are not members of AARP.

The bar is a bit hard to find in the casino, so wander toward the big blue "Keno-Progressive" sign. Each bar stool location has a flat in the bar surface draw poker video machine. The players are often intense, and you are advised not to chatter with those so engrossed. The bartenders are friendly but careful not to interrupt play. They are also, as is a Native American custom, extremely solicitous of senior citizens.

The main drawback here is the cacaphony of the nearby slots. The action is hot and heavy, and the sound effects make you feel like you're sitting near a calliope. I'm just a sucker (and I telegraph my Pennsylvania heritage in the process) for any Northwoods spot that runs specials on Rolling Rock.

If you're lucky enough to arrive at an off time and there's a Stockbridge tribal member behind the bar, you just might get to hear a few Munsee/Mohican legends. The tribe has an interesting history, with story traditions that trace back to New England and the mid-Atlantic states. See if you can get anyone to talk of the Ohdohs, a ghost tribe that some say followed the Mohicans on their trail of travails. Or you might hear a story about the American Revolution; the Stockbridge reservation has more descendants of that hallowed war for indepedence than any other Native American community of its size west of the Appalachians.

▼ ▼ ▼ ▼ ▼ ▼ ▼ ▼ ▼ ▼ ▼ ▼ ▼ ▼ ▼ ▼ ▼ ▼

Green Bay
Cock & Bull Publick House
1237 Main Street
(920) 432-1885

The C and B is a Main Street institution in Green Bay. Main Street is the rough equivalent of Madison's State Street or Milwaukee's Water Street. Out-of-towners start in this neighborhood because of its proximity to the downtown hotels and conference centers.

A few words about Main Street. It is an eclectic collection of generally youthful bars, pizza parlors, strip clubs, coffeehouses, shot-and-beer joints, at least one Latin music club, and a bar for alternative scenes. Many consider the C and B the crown jewel of the street.

While we are at it, mention should also be made of Green Bay's fragmented and evolving tavern scene. Broadway at one time had a solid six blocks of bars, but these were hit hard by urban renewal. Neighborhood bars are widely dispersed. The "downtown" is more the province of hotel/motel lounges. So Main Street is your best bet for a compact pub crawl.

The C and B is a spacious establishment with a well-appointed bar, an abundance of pool tables, and a design that encourages mingling. The look is a combination of traditional tavern flavor with brassier modern club elements. It is often crowded, especially on Friday and Saturday nights. Despite the heavy traffic, this nightspot is well kept and the service is prompt.

Its ads boast a beer list of over 200 selections, but the posting on brands is not always clear, and it could use some compact printed lists throughout the bar area. About eight taps are rotated on a seasonal basis. The current favorites are the home team selections from Hinterland. That brewery's Pub Draft, served up through this bar's nitrogen-charged tap, is as creamy a malt concoction as can be found this side of a root beer float. C and B's is one of the leading purveyors of this beer. It also stocks a collection of top-shelf liquor.

The ambience here is upscale pool hall, with multiple tables in action and an abundance of players. A warning to the guys: don't assume that you're going to teach the gals here your cue and table moves. There are some good women pool players here and you just might get hustled.

▼ ▼ ▼ ▼ ▼ ▼ ▼ ▼ ▼ ▼ ▼ ▼ ▼ ▼ ▼ ▼ ▼ ▼

Green Bay

Titletown Brewing
200 Dousman Street
(920) 437-2337

This old railroader is a soft touch for an old depot brewpub even if its roots are Chicago and Northwestern rather than my beloved Milwaukee Road. This is a great location, with train, ship, barge, and drawbridge action for the rubberneckers among you beer fans. Oh, by the way, there's this place across the street called Green Bay Brewing, so this is a beer lovers' doubleheader.

But back to the business at hand, which is beer and food in a delightful setting. This has become my favorite spot to eat in this quadrant of the state and the kitchen effort shows as much diligence as the brewroom. They render an admirable update on the Friday night fish fry, with plenty of choices for the non-batter inclined.

Still it was beer which brought me in here and beer that keeps me coming back. The brew schedule is as busy as the depot was in its prime. The "scheduled arrivals" are as follows: 400 Honey Ale, Railyard Amber Ale, Old Fort Howard Pale Ale, Bridge Out Stout, Johnny Blood Irish Red, and Befuddelator Doppelbock. The "special runs" as seasonals include the local favorite Grid Iron Gold and my nominees, a Belgian triple and an English ale called Mojo's Mile.

The bar gets regular traffic and it's fairly easy to strike up a beer-related conversation. The bar staff has always been sharp, friendly, and knowledgeable. Though one part of me misses the long gone dives of nearby Broadway, Titletown represents remarkable upgrade. All aboard!

▼ ▼ ▼ ▼ ▼ ▼ ▼ ▼ ▼ ▼ ▼ ▼ ▼ ▼ ▼ ▼ ▼

Keshena

War Bonnet
Highway 47 and 55
(715) 799-4335

Nestled on the southern edge of the internationally renowned Menominee reservation forest and a stone's throw from the Wolf River, the War Bonnet is one of the few pit stops along the Wolf. The ambience combines the country-and-western feel common in rural bars with the local tribal culture. You won't find many other spots where a lively discussion about the Crandon mine and water quality can rage among half the patrons while the other half watch *Dukes of Hazard* reruns. However, if you feel the need to debate treaty rights, spearfishing, and the virtues of Christopher Columbus, this is not the spot for you.

This is a true reservation bar as one might experience out west, not a tourist and trinket stop. Wisconsin reservations do not have many bars, and tribal elders often raise objections to alcohol consumption. This means that you need to value the atmosphere and not crave amenities. Standard national beers and a few regionals wet the whistles of loggers and fishermen. Thursday night is dollar night and weekends bring DJs and bands.

Though short on my favorite brews, the Bonnet is well stocked on Northwoods lore. A good story requires that the listeners buy a round for the teller. Logging and outdoors stories find full earthy expression here, as do the Algonkian legends of the manitou in the various forms recalled by Potawatomi, Chippewa, and Menominee. One wizened source on a bar stool related an entire geography of spirits of the rapids and falls of the Wolf system.

In this very spot I heard a ghostly epic that spanned the full distance of the St. Lawrence and the Great Lakes, the full annals of French, English, and American history, and the timeless legends of intertribal battles. The tale was a chilling cocktail of an errant Iroquois spirit, a doomsday device, and a parable of illicit moonshine. Potent stuff, with or without the shot and a beer.

Marinette

Rail House Brewing Company
2029 Old Peshtigo Road
(715) 732-4646

The rail theme here is not the only reason to toot your whistle. The drive to Marinette is rewarded with four solid house brews: Rail House Silver (a light ale), Gold Rush Red (a caramel malt ale), Coal Car Stout, and Pilsner Honey. Rail House kettles are also used to brew a variety of seasonal ales and a homemade root beer.

Then there's the food. Four appetizers, soups, salads, pasta, steaks, chicken, subs, and an extensive pizza selection. Oh, on Friday, the menu switches over to perch, walleye, cod, shrimp, and whitefish. The dessert selection is growing, too. And Rail House delivers the entire menu within the Marinette, Peshtigo, and Menominee (Michigan) area.

The Rail House may not rank with some of the brand-spanking-new palatial brew pubs of Milwaukee and Chicago, but it has come by its reputation honestly in the hardscrabble Northwoods. Some would say it's the only spot for good beer between Eagle River/Minocqua/Boulder Junction and Green Bay. The Rail House pulls in the travelers and serves as a local rallying point for beer fans.

The cultural milieu is pure transition zone. Marinette keeps one eye on the Fox Valley and the other on the Upper Peninsula of Michigan. Same here with the customers. A conversation here can ramble through the details of a shopping trip to Packer City's Port Plaza, the latest release of the regional music comedy group Da Yoopers, and the latest walleye fishing innovations.

The proposition that good locally brewed beer brings out the nostalgia in folks is borne out here. Among the self-defined regulars I found antique-car restorers, historic reenactors, farm equipment collectors, rendezvous participants, and builders of authentic bark canoes.

Many of my sources pointed to the Rail House as the best beer purveyor betwixt Green Bay and Marquette, Michigan. That compliment damns with faint praise. As hockey fans know, the drive from Green Bay to Marquette is a long one, with plenty of bars but few standouts. There are a few worthy rustics on the Michigan stretch of Highway 41. The Wisconsin passage from the mouth of the Fox to the Oconto and Peshtigo precincts has but a few serviceable bars. Rail House has little competition on the west side of the bay, though it would hold its own in the state's more blessed regions.

▼ ▼ ▼ ▼ ▼ ▼ ▼ ▼ ▼ ▼ ▼ ▼ ▼ ▼ ▼ ▼

Ron's Brick Tap
317 N. Central Avenue
(715) 384-5535

Any tavern that can certify, as Ron's does, that the tap lines are clean deserves an "A" for effort on behalf of quality draft beer. But customer satisfaction is a major priority here. That could be one reason that the place fills up after work and in the evenings.

The other reasons might have something to do with the customer-tailored beers. Why else would it offer specials on Dempsey's Pale Ale half liter, 16-ounce Budweiser specials, and buck-and-a-quarter Rolling Rock? How else would you account for a four-person order of bottled Guinness, Bass, Corona, and Labatt's Blue? What other explanation could be offered for a large assortment of shorties, including nonalcoholic varieties?

Bartenders at Ron's earn their keep at peak times. They need to deftly sling Rumple Minze shots, Leinie's, and cocktails for a mixed golf, NASCAR, and beer fan crowd. Eight tap lines include some nationals but reserve space for requests, test runs, and flavors of the month. They educate beer palates by introducing folks to the Central Waters brews.

Strangers are not left out at Ron's. The regulars won't let you remain nameless for long. Expect inquiries about your business, politics, and ancestry. If the usual crowd is in fine form, expect some strong opinions about government boondoggles and intrusive regulations.

You might guess that such a place would be ripe with good-natured hyperbole and leg pulling. You would be guessing right. Regulars often play a game of "gotcha" with new faces. In this variation of the game, newcomers are lured into conversation about their interests and accomplishments only to find a rejoinder from the bar from somone who's done it better or faster or knows more about it. This is a funny exercise if done without malice. It's insufferable if the know-it-alls believe they really do know it all.

During my visits the talk tended toward racing and golf. Both crowds are down-to-earth, with no pretense of pro status. Come October, they like a scary story or two. See if you can get someone started on the Upham Mansion tale.

▼　▼　▼　▼　▼　▼　▼　▼　▼　▼　▼　▼　▼　▼　▼　▼　▼

Minocqua

Otto's Beer and Brat Garden
509 Oneida Street
(715) 356-6134

Like so many Wisconsin spots, Otto's operates on a seasonal routine that tracks the ebb and flow of visitor trade and the recreational modes marked by the seasons. In summer it can be packed with tourists and in winter it becomes a subdued spot for calm sipping. Spring and fall are tougher to predict and depend a lot on whether the lakes are still frozen or whether early snow had knocked the leaves down before color peak.

Otto's itself is a lot of different things rolled into one. It's part in-town lodge, with the woodwork and fireplace we expect up north. It's part German gasthaus and stube and does not lack for Teutonic feel. But it's also an outpost where beer lovers on their way to Ashland and beyond must stop to pay homage.

During the summertime the beer list can creep up to 80 varieties. In the winter the offerings can fall off to a couple dozen, but with well-rounded representation in any season. The usual selections include varieties from Gray's, New Glarus, Point, Leinie's, Spaten, DAB, Hacker Pschorr, Becks, Bass, Harp, and Guinness. A vast improvement on the Pabst and Blatz out in the lake cottage bars.

But if you want to visit some of those while you're in the area then Otto's is a good base of operations from which to explore Oneida and Vilas counties. Customers and staff have steered me to some secluded rental cabins. Who knows, they might just point you in the direction of that mom and pop shack-tavern in the back country that tempts you with a "for sale" sign.

▼ ▼ ▼ ▼ ▼ ▼ ▼ ▼ ▼ ▼ ▼ ▼ ▼ ▼ ▼ ▼ ▼

Virgie Hunter's Bar
2097 South Road (off Highway X)
(715) 693-3532

Bottles of Point beer for $1. Just about everybody drinks it. Requests for other beers might bring strange looks from the regulars. Enough said. Those unfamiliar with the area might be fooled by the address. This is as rural a tavern as you will find this side of Wyoming. It's in a belt of rural taverns that starts where Stevens Point's 2nd Street turns into Highway X and runs north toward Schofield. *Be warned: This is a hard place to find unless you pick up the sign on Highway X.*

Alternately known as Virgie's, Hunter's, South Road Tavern, and Virgie Hunter's Bar, the Depression-era building has undergone few changes in 60 years and four different owners. It's still a DNR registration station that ear tags 1,200 deer a year, it still sells hunting licenses. The same Racine, Kenosha, and Milwaukee hunting families visit Grandpop's old spot and sometimes sleep in their trucks in the parking lot.

Fresh produce is available from a large on-site garden. A more or less continuous garage sale is going on out the side door (unless the garage is needed for Packer tailgate parties or Tupperware bingo). Hearty chicken soup and chili are available in the cooler months. The big annual event is a wild turkey and pheasant feed around Labor Day.

Maybe what impressed me the most during my visits was the complete lack of whining that is so common in rural taverns. No conspiracy theories about the DNR or the federal government. No trumped-up complaints about Indians, casinos, and spearfishing. The proprietors are busy having a good time running a bar. Even their terrier happily prances behind the bar in Virgie's.

This spot is a storyteller's delight. I have personally heard more ghost stories, pioneer legends, and contemporary tall tales here than in any other tavern in the state. This is the place where I picked up the leads to such stories as "Polonia's Polutnitsha," "Walter the Warden," and "Deer Camp Dick". The place may seem parochial but usually includes people who have hunted and fished the northern half of Wisconsin and know its back roads well.

One patron told me that an elderly man would appear in the parking lot years ago and sing in Polish to his wife inside. It was a song begging her to come home. The couple are long dead, but the twinkly eyed carrier of the tale said that some nights one can still hear that Polish song.

Oh, by the way, if you happen by at 8 or 9 A.M. on an autumn day you just might find the place packed.

▼ ▼ ▼ ▼ ▼ ▼ ▼ ▼ ▼ ▼ ▼ ▼ ▼ ▼ ▼ ▼ ▼ ▼

Peshtigo

The River Pub

French and Front Streets (Highway 41)
(715) 582-2900

The River Pub (known as La Valley's until recently) is an honest-to-goodness after-work bar for locals in an area brimming with hunting and fishing taverns. It also has the best intergenerational mix in this corner of the state. But if you want to hear old-timers spin yarns about the Peshtigo fire, you'd best stop by midafternoon.

The choices here are simple: ice-cold Miller or ice-cold Bud. Well, if you press the point, they might go to a back cooler and drag out an ancient can of Old Style. Despite that, it's still one of the better taverns on the Green Bay–Marinette run. Establishment sensibilities are telegraphed by the house specialty: ice-cold shots of schnapps.

The River Pub has a bit of the feel of a border state bar: slightly hard-edged but definitely not hard-ass, and pleasantly rowdy when in peak form. An earthy utterance or two should not surprise the visitor. Just plug the jukebox and bring up a mix of country, heavy metal, golden oldies, and adult contemporary tunes.

The oval bar is one of the biggest encountered outside of metropolitan areas. It's vintage Formica but remarkably unscathed by cigarette burns. Speaking of cigarettes, the River Pub is definitely a smoker's bar, but with sufficient ventilation to go easy on the noncombustible among us.

My friends swear by the fishing advice they pick up in these friendly confines. According to them, they have run into deepwater devotees, fly-fishers, smelters, river run fanatics, and those who ply the interior muskie lakes. Not to worry, they allow us lowly worm and bluegill types into their exalted space. On my autumn visits the place is more of a hunters' bar, with the blaze orange three deep at the bar. The regulars moan that they are displaced by the downstate crowd. One Fond du Lac wag proudly proclaimed that enough of his work buddies were in the joint to have a quorum for his union local.

▼ ▼ ▼ ▼ ▼ ▼ ▼ ▼ ▼ ▼ ▼ ▼ ▼ ▼ ▼ ▼ ▼

Rhinelander
Bugsy's Brown Street Pub and Sports Bar
16 N. Brown Street
(715) 369-2100

Wisconsin "sports bars" seem to encompass everything from the mom-and-pop ten-stool joint with 21-inch TV and Packers pennant to corporate-held big-screen multiplexes. Bugsy's does the TV route with eight screens and ups the ante in its huge space. This is a sports bar in which most sports could be played. And they do play indoor basketball and volleyball here.

So now you're thinking this is one of those glorified pool halls inhabited by Coors Light–drinking 20-somethings. Wrong! Bugsy's has a state-of-the-art four-barrel pub-brewing system. So far they've turned out a wheat, a dunkel, an amber, and a stout—with more on the way. Four additional taps are devoted to micros from around the region. And I suppose the bartenders might be able to rustle up some nationally known facsimile beer for the beer ambivalent.

Open only since July 1998, Bugsy's is well on its way to becoming a regional kind of "House on the Rock" of Northwoods bars that has to be seen to be believed. Local beer fanciers predict a bright future if Wisconsin gets a couple of snowy winters in a row to bring the snowmobilers and cross-country skiers back to the northeast.

The regulars include many recreation-savvy natives. A fishing guide kept my interest for a good hour, even though his story strayed over Hayward way to the famed guide Louis Number One and famed client Ted Williams. While I was thus engaged, my pals got the lowdown on the best housekeeping cottages and boat rentals.

While I mourn the loss of many of the venerable Northwoods taverns, with their yellowed linoleum and their desiccated and dust-fuzzy beef jerky, Bugsy's may represent a new trend that could get younger families back in the taverns. Just like back in those Eisenhower "happy days," only in the twenty-first century.

▼ ▼ ▼ ▼ ▼ ▼ ▼ ▼ ▼ ▼ ▼ ▼ ▼ ▼ ▼ ▼ ▼

Rhinelander

Labor Temple Bar
2 E. Anderson Street
(715) 848-3320

Here's a feisty little bar that opens at 11 A.M. and closes when there are no thirsty customers left. From the moment I went to work on this guidebook, it was my intent to include a union hall bar. Conventional wisdom would have pointed toward selection of the bigger spots in Racine, Madison, Neenah-Menasha, and Eau Claire. But time and time again my friends in organized labor pointed me toward this Northwoods outpost.

The union hall bar was once a standard part of every mill and factory town. Deindustrialization of many urban cores and flight of many workers to the suburbs left the labor halls as spots used for periodic meetings, not seven-day-a-week community centers. But not so in Rhinelander.

The Rhinelander Labor Temple Bar does a steady business as a tavern while serving that community function. Meetings adjourn to, and informally continue in, the bar.

It's the type of place where candidates for public office have to stop and show a steady gaze and a firm handshake. It's the type of place where traveling union officials must show their mettle by keeping up, beer for beer, with their members and run a tab in lieu of a dues rebate. A segment of Wisconsin's labor movement is in the capable hands of a number of working-class stalwarts, big guys with evidence of their time at the bar hanging unabashedly over their belts. They've seen all the union hall bars from Kenosha to Superior. They say this is the best. You don't want to argue with them.

Conversation is lively and of a populist political bent. If you're hungry, there's pizza. If you're thirsty, there's cold beer (nothing fancy). For itchy feet, there's a band every Saturday night. And if you have high-level recreation needs, there's an indoor golf machine.

Jimmy Hoffa wouldn't drink here, but John L. Lewis would.

ANOTHER ROUND

Wisconsin Breweries

Call for tour and special event information.

Capital Brewery (Garten Brau)
7734 Terrace Avenue
Middleton
(608) 836-7100
www.capital-brewery.com

City Brewing Company, LLC
1111 S. Third Street
La Crosse
(608) 785-4820

Esser's Cross Plains Brewery
2109 Hickory Street
Cross Plains
(608) 798-3911

Gray's Brewing Company
2424 West Court
Janesville
(608) 752-3552
www.graybrewing.com

Harbor City Brewing Company
535 W. Grand Avenue
Port Washington
(262) 284-3118
www.harborcitybrewing.com

Hinterland Brewing Company
313 Dousman Street
Green Bay
(920) 438-8050

▼ ▼ ▼ ▼ ▼ ▼ ▼ ▼ ▼ ▼ ▼ ▼ ▼ ▼ ▼ ▼ ▼ ▼ ▼

Jacob Leinenkugel Brewing Company
1 Jefferson Street
Chippewa Falls
(715) 723-5558

Jacob Leinenkugel Brewing Company
1515 N. Tenth Street
Milwaukee
(414) 931-3900

Joseph Huber Brewing Company (Berghoff)
1208 Fourteenth Avenue
Monroe
(608) 325-3191

Lakefront Brewery
1872 N. Commerce Street
Milwaukee
(414) 372-8800
www.lakefront-brewery.com

Miller Brewing Company
3939 W. Highland Boulevard
Milwaukee
(414) 931-2000

New Glarus Brewing Company
Highways W and 69
New Glarus
(608) 527-5850

Nicolet Brewing Company
2299 Brewery Lane
Florence
(715) 528-5244

Oconomowoc Brewing Company
750 E. Wisconsin Avenue
Oconomowoc
(262) 560-0388

Pioneer Brewing Company
320 S. Pierce Street
Black River Falls
(715) 284-7553

Slab City Brewing LLC
W3590 Pit Lane
Bonduel
(715) 758-2337

▼ ▼ ▼ ▼ ▼ ▼ ▼ ▼ ▼ ▼ ▼ ▼ ▼ ▼ ▼ ▼ ▼ ▼

Sprecher Brewing Company
701 W. Glendale Street
Glendale
(414) 964-2739
www.sprecherbrewery.com

Stevens Point Brewery LLC
2617 Water Street
Stevens Point
(715) 344-9310

Tyranena Brewing Company
1025 Owen Street
P.O. Box 736
Lake Mills
(920) 648-8699

Viking Brewing Company
234 Dallas Street
Dallas
(715) 837-1824
www.vikingbrewing.com

▼　▼　▼　▼　▼　▼　▼　▼　▼　▼　▼　▼　▼　▼　▼　▼　▼

Stevens Point

Witz End
1274 N. 2nd Drive
(715) 344-9045
www.thewitzend.com

The year 2001 brought change to this old rocking roadhouse. Beer fan and impresario Rick Borowitz handed over the Witz End reins to Betty Carmichael and Paul Schneider. My fondness for the place runs so deep that I just had to check in to see if the place is still in good hands. Not to worry, they're doing fine, and with expanded hours too.

The place retains its classic roadhouse setup. It's not as spacious as a big league nightclub or ballroom, but nevertheless has a great spatial arrangement for dancing, band watching, and sitting at the bar. So many of Wisconsin's best taverns are hampered on the entertainment front by angled rooms and neck-bending sightlines. For those of us who like to see the band and sip our beer, Witz End has the optimal arrangement.

Beer fans will be happy to know that beer treasures are still dispensed at this location. For many years this was the micro outpost of the central part of the state. They have good representation of just about all of Wisconsin's micros and regionals in bottles. Tapwise, they've always done well by the Central Waters brews. The tap rotation brings lots of seasonal treats. Several times I have sampled a seasonal New Glarus first at Witz End, a situation I caustically bring to the attention of my neighborhood tavern keepers when I remind them that Witz End is about 150 miles from New Glarus and we're only 20 miles from the brewery.

The only changes I've noticed so far at Witz End are some shifts in the age demographics. Rich Borowitz noted those trends under his regime as he and I commiserated about the aging process and how it gets harder to roust one's bones off the sofa for bands that don't start their sound checks until 10:30 p.m. Betty and Paul are doing fine with their younger crowd and the place still jumps on weekend nights.

Only time will tell if the early evening regulars will maintain the tradition of beer talk, gossip, and yarn spinning. Back in the years of my first encounters with Witz End, there was an odd assortment of DNR employees, UW-Stevens Point students and faculty, farmers, and salespeople who would regale me with stories. But we're probably safe on that score too. The walls themselves have tales to tell at Witz End.

▼ ▼ ▼ ▼ ▼ ▼ ▼ ▼ ▼ ▼ ▼ ▼ ▼ ▼ ▼ ▼ ▼

Sturgeon Bay

Inn at Cedar Crossing Pub
3rd Avenue and Louisiana Street
(920) 743-4249

This carefully restored 1884 building came into its current reincarnation in 1986. Along the way it picked up a place on the National Register of Historic Sites and added food and drink to its routine in 1989. The pub side of the business came into its own as it expanded its microbrew offerings and began to offer a lighter pub menu distinct from the dining area (which has its own fine reputation).

The result is a restaurant-based bar that stands on its own. Customers, particularly in the busy Door County high season, do indeed come in just for drink and conversation. Draft offerings during my last visit included Paulaner Hefe-Weizen, Samuel Adams Summer Ale, and Bass Ale, though there is some seasonal variation. At last count, the bottled brews tallied up at 34 types, with good representation of imports and micros. Cedar Crossing Pub also has a following for its summer fruit and spirits drinks, often made with local fruit.

It is hard to find the tavern middle ground in Door County. Many good spots are overcome by the crush of tourists. Development and gentrification are claiming others. The Door County taverns of manure on barn boots, the smell of fish entrails, and boatmen's corncob pipes is disappearing. Many of the new spots, as improved as they are from a beer-drinking (and sanitary) perspective, are devoid of local flavor.

The Cedar Crossing Pub represents one aspect of the middle ground. Its downtown business district location helps it draw both travelers and locals. The talk ranges through local land use controversies, real estate prices, and construction industry woes. It is a conversational mix that is on the increase in Wisconsin, but in Door County it is probably more advanced than elsewhere.

One element of the Cedar Crossing Pub operation really impressed me: a congenial midafternoon crowd that makes for good casual companionship for sports or outdoors talk. Many of the best taverns are faced with the lunch and after-work rushes and deal with a lull in between. Some of the shot-and-a-beer joints have afternoon customers who are simply stretching lunchtime into bartime. What is nice about this spot is that it gets sufficient numbers of laid-back travelers to affirm the unhurried mood that befits Sturgeon Bay.

Tomahawk

Pik's Pub

8 W. Wisconsin St.
(715) 453-8966

L ocals swear by this nicely renovated and redecorated mainstay. It's earned the approval that goes with doubling up the tavern business with an informal community center status. The result is a Northwoods tavern look without the grime and odors that afflict many taverns. Standard Northwoods tavern decor is spoofed a bit by some unusual wall hangings and a mounted deer's rear end.

Pik's has grown beyond the limited-selection shot-and-beer place by the addition of nine taps. The focus is still on the big-boy corporate brews, but it's gradually teasing palates with Leinie's and Point. All indications point toward the eventual appearance of micros.

Especially if the music crowd holds up. Pik's serves as a multigenre venue for blues, rock, and country. Monday is the blues jam. Wednesdays and Fridays are the primary band nights. Among the entertainment functions are periodic fund-raising dances to buy musical instruments for local students.

The best compliment I can pay Pik's is that it's geared to its local customer base, not some mythic tourist profile of what flatlanders with bucks would like. That is exactly the reason many travelers will like it; it's natural in its place and not pretending to be something it's not. This is the whole lure of the Northwoods tavern, to not be a stranger when you walk in the very first time and to not be surrounded by painfully obvious tourists. Otherwise, you might as well hang out at bars in the Dells and pretend you're in the Boundary Waters.

Tomahawk itself is a fair to middling community for a Northwoods pub crawl, both in the city and in its environs. Some of my hardier associates include it on a tour that takes in Merrill and Marathon City to the south. If you do make that loop, be sure to hit the spots on Highway 107 on the west side of Merrill and the little bunker of a tavern at the junction of Lincoln County highways E and M. Let me know what you find, I've been meaning to stop for years.

▼ ▼ ▼ ▼ ▼ ▼ ▼ ▼ ▼ ▼ ▼ ▼ ▼ ▼ ▼ ▼ ▼ ▼ ▼ ▼

ANOTHER ROUND
Beer and Bar Reading

Breweries of Wisconsin, Jerry Apps, University of Wisconsin Press, Madison, 1992.

Cream City Suds, PO Box 1251, Milwaukee, WI 53201, (414) 645-1580 (bimonthly)

Great Lakes Brewing News, 214 Muegel Road, East Amherst, NY 14051, (716) 689-5841 (bimonthly)

Midwest Beer Notes, PO Box 237, Ridgeland, WI 54763, (715) 837-1120 (bimonthly)

▼ ▼ ▼ ▼ ▼ ▼ ▼ ▼ ▼ ▼ ▼ ▼ ▼ ▼ ▼ ▼ ▼ ▼

Wausau

Scott Street Steak and Pub
124 Scott Street
(715) 842-2424

The conversion from downtown beer and sandwich joint to regional blues and brews spot was done the old-fashioned way: they earned it. Still, the midday traffic has its share of business lunches, and 5 o'clock brings an after-work crowd. The Saturday afternoon crowd, on the other hand, includes many travelers. The regulars include quite a few downtown office workers and government employees. The evenings bring a mix of brew fans, sports enthusiasts, and music lovers. More on the music in a bit.

What brings in the traffic off Highway 51? For starters, eight tap heads with variable offerings of solid Wisconsin microbrews such as Gray's and Sprecher. Summit and Leinie's seasonals often round out the draft selection, along with the locally popular Foster's. The bottled selection usually tallies about two dozen micros and imports, with Gray's having a distinct following among repeat visitors headed toward lakeshore cottages.

Friday and Saturday nights bring out friendly crowds for music. Bookings run toward the blues, with forays into roots rock and fusion. Tony Brown and the Landing Crew make this their northern outpost, as do Otis and the Alligators and Reverend Raven and the Chain Smoking Altar Boys. This is a great tandem visit with Witz End in Stevens Point (and what the heck, with Holly Rocks in Wisconsin Rapids). For good times, these northcentral nightspots hold their own with Madison and Milwaukee.

The regulars include a number of trusty tavern scouts. This is one of the few spots where reliable sources can give you the overview on Wausau's neighborhood taverns. Their field intelligence extends out to nearby Rothschild, Schofield, and Wausau Junction. Rumor has it that they also have the lowdown on hotspots for cribbage and sheepshead.

Scott Street Pub has a comfortable saloon feel with its no-frills interior, bison head over the bar, and old-time pinball machine. Its extensive sandwiches and appetizer menu merits sampling. Don't miss the onion rings.

▼ ▼ ▼ ▼ ▼ ▼ ▼ ▼ ▼ ▼ ▼ ▼ ▼ ▼ ▼ ▼ ▼ ▼

Wisconsin Rapids

Holly Rocks
114 Second Street North
(715) 423-1800

A favorite stop for music fans in central Wisconsin, Holly Rocks is also a beer-drinking haven. The seven taps seem like a modest number until you see the handles marked for Hacker Pschorr and the Central Waters brews. The bottled selection is impressive, with most regionals and the rarely seen Tennents from Scotland.

This bar has a heart that beats to music, be it blues, classic rock, bluegrass, folk rock, or reggae. The decor follows the theme with suspended and wall-hanging guitars, saxophones, trumpets, banjos, and trombones. A nice collection of vintage concert posters and recording artist photos grace the walls, with nostalgia evoked for the Doors, Hendrix, the Who, Elvis, Janis Joplin, and Bob Marley, among others.

Many music clubs are short on conversation, but not Holly Rocks. On non–band nights the place can be as talkative as any neighborhood tavern. Much of the conversation runs to music. Or should I say life and music? One dueling trivia duo treated me to a run-through of music from the 60s and 70s and its relationship to movies, advertising, television, sports, and high school reunions.

Frequent patrons make the case that there is an emerging folklore of music clubs. In their view the sagas of spaced-out roadies, internal band spats, and seduction by song is the stuff of legends. They made convincing arguments with the archetypes of classic myth, the emerging historical sensibilities of rock and roll, the passage of the five decades since rockabilly, and even a ghost story or two.

Friendly crowds and even friendlier bartenders are the norm. They'll cheerfully steer you to other good taverns (see Huey's Pub and Eatery). A big picture window with a view of a little park and the Wisconsin River lets you watch the world go by. Some might argue that Holly Rocks is a nightclub, but its satisfied beer drinkers say otherwise.

Oh, did I mention that this is one of the cleanest and best-maintained bars I've ever seen? Yet it doesn't come off as a prissy place; the earthy crowd and funky CD collection see to that. It's unusual to hear such mixed conversations about microbrews, guitar chords, sound systems, and album critiques. Check out the odd ashtray collection!

▼ ▼ ▼ ▼ ▼ ▼ ▼ ▼ ▼ ▼ ▼ ▼ ▼ ▼ ▼ ▼ ▼ ▼

Index of Places and Events

Page numbers in boldface indicate the taverns' main listing.

▼ ▼ ▼ ▼ ▼ ▼ ▼ ▼ ▼ ▼ ▼ ▼ ▼ ▼ ▼ ▼ ▼ ▼